Media in Ireland: The Sea

MEDIA IN IRELAND

THE SEARCH FOR DIVERSITY

EDITED BY

Damien Kiberd

OPEN AIR

Set in Janson for
OPEN AIR
an imprint of Four Courts Press
Fumbally Lane , Dublin 8, Ireland
e-mail: info@four-courts-press.ie
and in North America
Four Courts Press, c/o ISBS,
5804 N.E. Hassalo Street, Portland,
Oregon 97213, USA

A catalogue record for this title
is available from the British Library.

ISBN 1-85182-315-8

Printed in Ireland
by Betaprint Ltd, Dublin

Contents

Notes on contributors

Professor Joe Lee is Professor of History at University College, Cork, and a columnist with the *Sunday Tribune*.

Bob Collins is Director-General of RTE.

Damien Kiberd is editor of the *Sunday Business Post*.

Dr Brian Feeney, a columnist with the *Irish News* and a lecturer in history, was a Belfast City Councillor for the SDLP from 1981 to 1993.

David Begg is General Secretary of the Communications Workers' Union.

Colm Rapple is a freelance journalist and a former Group Business Editor of both the Irish Press Group and Independent Newspapers.

Joanna Bogle is a journalist and a broadcaster with the BBC World Service and the author of historical biographies.

Introduction

DAMIEN KIBERD

Is it possible that a true plurality of views could find expression within Irish print and broadcast media? Can the mass media simultaneously operate to a commercial mandate while making media products more democratic, inclusive, and accountable in their methods? Will journalists become the masters or the slaves of new technology? Will the development of a global TV culture inevitably reduce the level of public debate in Ireland? And can Irish journalists begin to apply more thought and consideration to the editorial decisions they take and the ethical choices they make in their daily work?

These are just some of the important questions dealt with in this volume, which examines a number of major issues facing journalists, editors, and indeed the owners of media companies in a rapidly changing media environment.

The scope of the book is broad. It asks if the concept of public service broadcasting can survive in an era where the acceptance of the 'pay-per-view' principle gains in strength, *en route* providing a small number of multinational corporations with enormous cash flow and profit. It explores whether it will be possible to sustain and justify investment in quality programming if the introduction of digital TV deeply fragments national and global TV audiences *(Collins,* pp 23ff).

In his contribution, Professor Joe Lee (pp 10ff) examines the impact of imported TV culture on Ireland, which he sees as promoting an intolerant value system of no-fault individualism. He also examines the absence of balance in important debates conducted on our own public service broadcasting system. He concludes that we may have passed from 'the sometimes suffocating certainties of Catholic Church teaching . . . to the equally suffocating certainties of anti-Catholic teaching of today without ever ascending to the phase of genuinely liberal democratic inquiry'.

The volume examines the increasing concentration of media ownership, and the implications that this may have for the work of individual journalists and the preservation of unique cultures and identities. The process of concentration and of cross-ownership between information companies is both global and local and is quite rapid (*Begg*, pp 59ff). Ideally, technological advances would further empower the individual in society and improve the internal and external relationships of a society, but in reality they may merely create powerful global entities that are answerable to no government and which may indeed subvert the regulatory role of any government, no matter how powerful.

Concentration of ownership can, in certain circumstances, lead to a reduction in the diversity of views finding expression in the media. It can also reduce the range of employment options available to journalists and editors, and can promote a climate of self-censorship.

At their bleakest, current trends may lead to what Chomsky and Herman* describe as a media that serves to 'mobilise support for the special interests that dominate the state and private activity'.

With commentary replacing the strict reportage of fact in many newspapers and indeed on radio and television, the absence of a defined 'ethics of opinion' among media practitioners will raise fears of continuing and widespread bias. Again to quote Chomsky and Herman, this bias may arise from 'the pre-selection of right thinking people, internalised preconceptions and the adaptation of personnel to the constraints of ownership, organisation, market, and political power'.

The book also looks at the areas of society which enjoy only limited access to the mass media (*Rapple*, pp 68ff), and asks if a more inclusive commercial philosophy could be created and sustained either through different modes of media regulation and taxation, or through state intervention, with all its attendant dangers. The possible cross-subsidisation of identifiable media outlets is examined against the background of the experience of a number of developed economies.

This volume also gives an outsider's view (*Bogle*, pp 80ff) of the remarkable tensions that have emerged between Christian and indeed Catholic thinking on the one hand and major Irish media organisations on the other. The writer holds that these tensions have become so

---

* *Manufacturing Consent: The Political Economy of the Mass Media* (New York, 1988).

manic in some instances that the confessional role of the media may come to resemble that of the Church in other times. In the course of a lively contribution, the author provides some cautionary advice based on external experience which may be of permanent value to those who would see a role for the modern journalist as a social engineer. The message is that thoughtful journalism should not be afraid to demand of others that care and consideration is given to any plan to discard traditions which have served society well in the past.

Journalists, in general, try to make society more open and to make those who hold power more accountable. They are hampered in their work by a variety of factors: by legal constraints, by lack of resources, and by self-censorship. Around them, batteries of better-resourced people seek to filter the information reaching them and to package it in certain, often contrived, ways (*Feeney*, pp 41ff).

But journalists are frequently their own worst enemies, too. They tend to travel in packs, they cluster around the flame of a cloying consensus, they close their minds to ideas they sometimes do not want to hear. Sometimes they cut corners in the pursuit of demanding editorial or commercial objectives. And above all, there seems to be a secular (that is, long term) tendency to alter the nature of journalism in a manner that places reduced emphasis on the reportage of fact and greater emphasis on the culture of comment. In this situation, journalists and what they produce are likely to become the subject of great controversy in the coming period (*Kiberd*, pp 33ff).

This volume of papers, presented at the Sixth Cleraun Media Conference (see p. 88), seeks to provoke a deeper analysis of what is happening to the Irish media, of the good developments and of those that are less welcome. Inter alia, it may help to point a new way forward to Irish journalists, editors, and the owners of media organisations. Such an approach could lead to a greater sense of diversity within the media and allow journalists to emerge with enhanced credibility from a period of stark change in this most vital sector of our public life.

Democracy and public service broadcasting in Ireland

JOE LEE

Icannot speak with any professional authority on broadcasting, or any type of media, except as an occasional contributor to programmes or columns. I am interested in the media because of the crucial role it must play in fostering a vibrant democracy, and indeed a vibrant society, in any country. Contrary to fashionable claims, it is not that the Republic of Ireland has lacked an intellectual tradition. What it has lacked is a tradition of intellectual debate. In my view, the prime purpose of public service broadcasting ought to be to provide a forum conducive to fostering a tradition of vigorous, open, pluralistic debate. I realise that to approach the question in this way is to ignore a great deal of what most of us look for on television. Many of us simply want to be entertained. Even here, however, it is becoming increasingly difficult to avoid the wider implications of private sector control. Many people watch more sport than anything else on television, but now media monopolies and/or pay-per-view television pose a real challenge to the public. Sport has become so central to questions of identity, and of participation in civic discourse around the world, that equal access to mass sporting occasions on television—certainly where teams or individuals from one's own country are concerned—can be reasonably regarded as a right of citizenship. I won't linger on this at present, beyond noting that it is an issue that is likely to grow in importance as sport becomes ever more prominent as part of what we are.

The main ideological issue discussed in the Green Paper on Broadcasting concerns the balance to be struck between market criteria and public service criteria. I am a strong believer in the principle of competition, wherever this can occur without detriment to more fundamental values. Competition is not an end in itself. As a means to an end, it helps keep all of us on our toes in a variety of ways. There are few human activities that cannot benefit from the spur of competition.

But when competition becomes a value in itself, as distinct from a means to an end, it can be enormously destructive. To be constructive, competition must be channelled. The basic question for me is how does one channel the potential of the media, and of television in particular, to enhance the quality of our national performance in general, and of our democracy in particular.

It may be argued that any state attempt to channel television is itself contrary to democratic principle. Is not the idea of a free market central to modern democracy? The free market can certainly be a powerful solvent of anti-democratic privileges. But it can also create dangerous anti-democratic privileges. The market in ideas is not the same as the market in goods. For one thing, there would have to be absolute equality of access to the media market for democratic equality to be achieved. But equality of access does not exist. In this respect democracy and capitalism are not necessarily identical. They can even be mutually exclusive. There can be no blanket generalisations about this, for all depends on the circumstances of the individual state. Discussion of the role of public service broadcasting in Ireland must therefore focus on our specific circumstances.

We are one of the most peculiarly situated states in the entire media cosmos. As one of the smallest English-speaking states in the world, with exceptionally close personal ties to England and America, we are uniquely open to the impact of international television, which is dominated by English, American, and, to some extent, Australian, concepts of what constitutes television culture. There is no other state in quite the same situation. It has been suggested that Ireland occupies the same position in relation to Britain as Canada occupies in relation to the United States. There are obvious similarities. But Ireland's position is nevertheless essentially different from Canada's. We are not just a small state beside a big one. We are also a formerly colonised people beside former colonial masters. Irish mindsets are influenced not only by geographical proximity, as Canadians are, but also by a historical experience that is quite different from that of Canada relative to the United States. Canada has also a highly conscious French-speaking culture, which obliges other Canadians to interrogate themselves, however reluctantly, about the nature of Canadian identity.

Our geographical, linguistic, cultural, and psychological location leaves us uniquely related to the most powerful media culture in the world. This offers opportunities, and poses threats. A vibrant, self-confident, self-reliant, culturally distinctive society, which has the ambition and the ability to take advantage of what is best and to reject what is worst, ought to be in a position to import a great deal, to blend it with its own native products, and become all the more vibrant a society thanks to the fruitful mixture. On the other hand, a small country in our circumstances, carrying the psychological baggage of an inferiority complex, may be in danger of succumbing to, rather than selecting from, the pressure of the international English-speaking media. If we have sufficient intellectual independence, then we can profit from our open access to the wider English language media world, and indeed make our own distinctive contribution to it. If we don't, we will inevitably become mere parrots, however eloquently we may mimic our masters.

The challenge of creating, and sustaining, intellectual independence in our circumstances is a formidable one. It is not that we are incapable of resisting patently propagandistic presentations of Anglo/American/Australian vintage at the expressly political level. Blatant propaganda is relatively harmless. It can be directly exposed. What is much more insidious, and far more difficult to cope with, is the infiltration of the silent value system about the nature of society that dominates the international media. That value system is essentially based on hedonistic, or no-fault, individualism. While mouthing the rhetoric of tolerance, it is essentially illiberal, rejecting pluralism in practice however much it preaches it in principle, and instinctively dismissing anyone who does not subscribe to its own ideology as intellectually and morally retarded. It is hardly an exaggeration to say that at least 90 per cent of the representatives of this media culture, whether producers, directors, presenters, script writers, or contributors, believe that personal gratification is the main touchstone of individual behaviour. This not only makes them advocates of behaviour such as divorce and abortion—to take the two issues central to the Irish debate on 'pluralism' —as a matter of principle, but makes it impossible for them even to conceive that any rational or intelligent creature could genuinely hold an alternative view.

This will inevitably be the case in media circles dominated by

Anglo-American assumptions. Individualists though they believe themselves to be, there will in fact be little individualism in their world view. The vast majority are virtually interchangeable clones in this regard. That is the nature of the beast, and will remain so unless conscious efforts are made to counteract it. In the Irish case it is reinforced by the feeling of a younger generation that it is fighting the good fight for liberation from the stifling orthodoxies of an earlier generation, particularly associated with the moral hegemony of Catholic Church teaching on sexuality, which the vast majority of media people appear to regard as repressive, either in terms of inhibiting their own lifestyles, or of conflicting with their self-image as intrepid crusaders for 'liberalism'. That disposition is an essential part of any lively media. But it becomes as stifling as any other orthodoxy when it achieves unquestioned dogmatic status among its disciples. That has become overwhelmingly the case with private sector television throughout the English-speaking world. Public service broadcasting offers a potential alternative. In Irish circumstances, it is virtually the only filter between us and the dominant value system of the international media, whether imported directly into Ireland or mediated through British and satellite television. Whether or not the potential can be realised is a different matter. This is where the issue of equality of access arises. Equality of access is the core issue. Without it, public service broadcasting is merely a façade behind which ideological bias can happily and self-righteously flourish—in the name of public service. Without equality of access, there can be no such thing as a democratic market in the world of ideas. There can only be a rigged market. Nor does access simply mean that different viewpoints among the public have adequate exposure. It does mean that. But it means, even more crucially, that the diversity of viewpoints within the station itself reflects the diversity of viewpoints among the public. It means that, on highly divisive issues, producers, presenters, and reporters broadly reflect the plurality of public perspectives. It means there can be no pervasive in-house ideology threatening to distort the overall public service perspective.

The 1995 divorce debate illustrated the problem quite clearly. RTE was naturally the main forum for that debate. But RTE was not a neutral forum. I am not here mainly concerned with the question of management decisions about the number of broadcasts allotted for the dif-

fering viewpoints. That does raise legitimate issues of fairness, but they
pertain to the functioning of the political process as a whole, and not in
the first instance to the functioning of RTE. The wider issue revolves
around the silent assumptions of programmers.

The vast majority of media people clearly supported the principle of
no-fault divorce. That is entirely their right as citizens. It is not, however, the right of a public service broadcasting organisation to address
so controversial an issue in an unbalanced manner. There would be no
difficulty in substantiating the view that there was an overwhelming
assumption on the part of RTE programmers that supporting no-fault
divorce was the correct response, and that opponents were either stu-
pid, or callous, or both. That is part and parcel of the political game.
But it is not part and parcel of public service broadcasting. Once it
becomes so, there is not much case for public service broadcasting. The
problem is not the personal opinions of the programmers. They are, of
course, as entitled to those as anybody else. The problem is the illusion
that their personal opinions do not influence the way they present
issues. This is all the more so if the nature of institutions tends to foster particular mindsets. It is even more so again if the institution
involved exerts a potentially disproportionate influence on public opinion. The influence of a mindset in a television station is potentially
vastly greater than in most other institutions. It is something akin to
having privileged access to a pulpit in the corner of every living room
in the country. It is therefore crucial in a society that purports to cherish democratic pluralism that the pulpit should not be programmed in
a particular direction. Of course RTE authorities would strenuously
deny that there was an RTE line on no-fault divorce. And they would
be right. There was no RTE line. There didn't have to be. Programme
makers had so internalised a value system conducive to no-fault divorce
that there was a *de facto* line, even while *de jure* the stance of the station
was no doubt correct. That is the most effective type of line of all.

A personal example must suffice. I myself appeared on only one discussion on divorce, a very brief one. I tried ineffectually to explain my
position, to the effect that I agreed with the need for divorce in certain
cases, particularly where either partner was demonstrably suffering
abuse, but that I was opposed to the principle of no-fault divorce on the
grounds that any responsible society had to hold individuals responsi-

ble for the consequences of their actions for others. The argument cut
no ice with anybody, least of all the interviewer, whose last question to
me was 'Professor Lee, are you still going to vote against divorce?', as if
it were inconceivable that so enlightened a creature as my good self
could possibly behave in so retarded a manner. And that particular
interviewer was as intelligent, as civilised, and as fair as one will find on
any programme. But it just didn't enter her mindset that there could be
any other way of looking at things. The influence of RTE on social values is not simply confined to programmes during situations of conflict.
Public opinion on the issue will inevitably be influenced by the
assumptions projected by programmers over the years. 'Mindsets' don't
start with a blank page at the beginning of a referendum campaign.
Views are conditioned by the manner of presentation even in relatively
quiet periods.

There are several steps that could be taken to ensure that public service broadcasting presents a balanced perspective on all major issues.
The first is the open and frank recognition that programmers, being
human, have prejudices and that even when they consciously seek to
control them, these will inevitably influence their approach.
Programmers no more stand outside the issues under discussion than,
for instance, historians or social scientists stand outside their subjects.
The difference is that in the academic world virtually every view will be
vigorously challenged by colleagues; progress emerges out of constant
criticism, of thesis and antithesis, proposition, reply, and rebuttal.
There is hardly any comparable challenging of colleagues within RTE.
Where highly divisive issues are involved—which in Irish circumstances means mainly in the areas of sexual morality, of Northern
Ireland, and of neutrality—it is pointless demanding that programmers
should not let their personal views intrude into their programmes. It is
also depriving the public of a right to know, in two senses.

Firstly, the public has a right to know the real views of the programmer. Secondly, several of the presenters and interviewers are themselves among the people most qualified to have views. They are among
the best minds in Irish public life—but they are in public life, not outside it. Instead of trying to pretend to a spurious impartiality, programmers should be allowed to freely indulge their preferences. But those
preferences should be openly on the line. Public service broadcasters

are not commentators on the game. They are players in the game. The principle of balance means little if it is simply confined to ensuring more or less equal time for contrary viewpoints, or a more or less equal number of public figures being lined up to express their conflicting views, unless this is also extended to the programmers themselves. If there is to be genuine balance within public sector broadcasting, then that balance must apply to interviewer as well as interviewed. Otherwise, a healthy pluralism cannot be guaranteed.

It is not easy to achieve balance, particularly given the depressing lack of diversity in the dominant viewpoints in the media, whether it be on television, on radio, or in newspapers. There is much preaching, but little practice, of pluralism. It is itself one of the ironies of Irish life that there should be so little pluralism of perspective in a media that constantly intones the virtues of pluralism. That seems to be almost inherent in the nature of the media itself, and poses particular problems for any public service institution that is supposed to serve all of the people and not merely the fashionable mindsets among the cliques of the day. RTE in this respect simply mirrors the fashions of the private sector media.

This has nothing to do with the intellectual calibre of the individuals involved. In my experience, that calibre is not just higher, but distinctly higher, among RTE personnel, on average, than in the English or American media. But RTE is itself the victim of the wider circumstances prevailing in Irish journalism. For whatever reason, there is little ongoing genuine debate about most issues in the Irish media. There is plenty of talk, but little real discussion. The mindsets of the participants are already fixed. Look at the opinion columns in the newspapers. A handful of commentators are worth reading because they are sufficiently unpredictable to be interesting. The reader cannot precisely predict their line on most matters without actually reading them. But in most cases, you can press a button and know what you are going to get before the content comes out. They are often very well written. Indeed, one can only admire the average level of literacy in the main opinion-oriented papers. But that is a different matter. Too many commentators seem to simply assume the superiority of their own version of revealed truth. Their columns are devoted to propounding the one true faith. Evidence is irrelevant in the face of doctrine.

Ireland seems to have passed from the sometimes suffocating certainties of Catholic Church teaching of a generation ago to the equally suffocating certainties of anti-Catholic teaching of today without ever ascending (and here of course my choice of language reveals my own ideological preferences) to the phase of genuinely liberal democratic inquiry. One orthodoxy strives to supplant another, both equally based on faith, both equally committed to the argument from authority, both determined to fit evidence into their framework of thinking, rather than adapt the framework to evidence. Ironically, the new orthodoxy is more authoritarian in its instincts and prescriptions in many respects than much Catholic teaching and practice as it is today, in contrast to what it was in an earlier generation.

When we use the current fashionable terms 'openness, transparency and accountability', we should apply them not only to politics in the narrow sense but also to the media. Every democratic society should interrogate itself continuously. The media is central to that ethos of interrogation. But the media is itself a central constituent component of society. It too requires interrogation. It is a matter of common observation that just as universities conduct research on virtually every branch of knowledge and every aspect of social activity, except universities, so does the media aspire to interrogate every major institution of society, except the media. One of the great weaknesses of 'traditional' society in Ireland was the dearth of effective mechanisms of self-interrogation. We are now in danger of moving from one system of uncritically received conventional wisdom to an alternative system of equally uncritically received conventional wisdom, produced and reproduced by preachers equally convinced of the correctness of their views, and equally prone to dismiss doubters as deviants or even heretics.

Given the dearth of genuinely intellectual discourse in the public culture, there is an inevitable temptation for even public service journalists to search for the 'scoop' as a substitute for systematic analysis. This pressure to get the 'scoop' was partly what led to RTE's embarrassment in the 'Tuffy case'. Equally instructive as RTE's role was the response of the private sector media to that particular 'scoop' before the gaffe was exposed. RTE was loudly praised for at last adopting the robust approach which had for too long been allegedly crushed out of them in this allegedly repressive society by axiomatically corrupt politicians. Concern with the patient search for truth was not self-evidently central to those commentaries. Nor did those who rushed to judgement make any attempt to interrogate themselves when the hoax was exposed within a day or two. Investigative journalism naturally considers confrontation, exposure, and denunciation as the name of the game. From the point of view of private sector mentalities, responding to the lure of profit, that is understandable. For public service broadcasters to embrace that ethos, however, raises far more fundamental questions about the nature both of society and of broadcasting.

I must stress, to preclude the danger of being misrepresented—or at least to have the statement on record in view of inevitable misrepresentation—that I do not believe in anything so vulgar as a conspiracy among journalists in general, or broadcasters in particular, to achieve a specific agenda, even the misleadingly termed 'liberal' agenda. Conspiracy is not the issue. The media would not be remotely as influential if the consensus in favour of the principle of an atomised society based on the value of no-fault individualism were the result of conspiracy. Precisely the fact that the media consensus on the superiority of that ideology is so pervasive means that a conspiracy is not necessary, even if it were desired.

The public tends to be suspicious, and rightly so, of information packaged by professional politicians as likely to be selective, self-serving, and misleading. But the public nowadays absorbs far more information from the media, and particularly from television, than from politicians. We have not yet adjusted our concept of education to take cognisance of the central role the media now plays in influencing our views. Indeed, many of the issues on the political agenda are set by the media. Government ministers regularly express more concern about the media response to issues than about the opposition's response in the Dáil. This is reasonable enough. They have ample mechanisms for dealing with the opposition. They do not have the same mechanisms, fortunately, for dealing with the media. But politicians, like everybody else, need media education. I am not talking here about how to present themselves on programmes. They can take professional advice on that. What I am talking about is how to evaluate the media. This is perhaps even more important for politicians than for other citizens. This is because they depend so heavily on the media for much of their information, and even for many of their ideas. Our parliamentary process is so underdeveloped that there are few research resources available in Leinster House. Politicians in general have few independent sources of information or evaluation. Ministers can no doubt draw on Civil Service advice but the vast majority of TDs have no access to that. They are therefore inclined to swallow what they hear on television, including documentaries, quite uncritically. Politicians, and the public at large, both need and deserve specific guidance on how to 'read' the media.

Media literacy has become a prerequisite for the healthy functioning of a participatory democracy. Evaluating the media means identifying, in the first instance, the value systems reflected in the way current affairs are presented. It may, of course, be claimed that there is already ample public evaluation of the media. Are there not regular columns on radio and TV in most newspapers? Is there not the very useful 'What it says in the papers' on 'Morning Ireland' and on Raidió na Gaeltachta? There are indeed, and they serve a useful purpose. But the purpose of 'What it says in the papers' is to inform rather than evaluate. And the regular radio and TV columns, while they frequently contain penetrating observations on individual programmes, are not intended to provide systematic evaluation of the value system of individual programmers. Needless to say, newspapers do not evaluate newspapers, even if occasional jousts occur between individual journalists. While the public can find any amount of critical commentary by the media on politicians daily, it will search in vain for critical commentary by the media on the media, even though the media is just as important a contributor—indeed, often more important—to public discourse in many respects as are the politicians.

The media will become even more important in the future in the formation of opinion. A generation ago the main influences on the moulding of mentalities were the family, the Church, and the school. The family is declining in influence, for a variety of reasons. The role of the Church is receding. Children still spend as much time in school, if not in the family or in church, but many of the values they learn at school are themselves derived from the media. And they themselves spend more time in front of the television than in front of the teacher over the course of a year. Television, reinforced by other media, will determine even more than at present the agenda for public discourse. Citizens need to learn how to evaluate media presentations, or they will become in large measure prisoners of the dominant assumptions of the media class. By media education for the masses, I don't mean teaching all of us how to 'do media', how to become a journalist, or a programmer. Only a tiny proportion of us can go in that direction. Relatively few of us, even with the highly desirable development of local media, can become media producers. But we are all media consumers. And nowhere else is consumer education so urgent. If we are concerned with the creation of an independently minded citizenry, this has to become central to our entire education system.

Media education ought not to be an optional extra at second level. Indeed, I would argue it ought not to be an optional extra at third level either, and I would have it play a central role in adult education. Adults of all ages, no less than the rising generation, need to be taught media literacy. Without media education, our proud boast that our younger generation is better educated than ever before loses some of its validity. Longer educated, yes. But better educated? Better educated for what? Hardly for citizenship, if they receive no guidance in how to evaluate the main source of their ideas for the rest of their lives. Education for citizenship today means, above all, education in media literacy. It can, no doubt, be argued that the curriculum is already tightly packed, that it is impossible to make space for yet another subject. But I am not talking here mainly about introducing another specialist subject, even though there is need for some element of that. But just as media presentation influences our perspectives on a whole range of issues, so the media dimension should pervade a whole range of subjects. Indeed, one way of combining traditional academic disciplines with the demand for 'relevance' could be precisely through the media dimension.

My own subject, history, could certainly acquire profitably a media dimension to its teaching. There can be few more effective ways of teaching pupils and students how to evaluate evidence—and the evaluation of evidence is central to historical education—than to expose them to media presentations, whether television, film, radio, newspaper or magazine, on historical topics, and teach them how to evaluate the use of evidence in the presentation. There has been a row already about Neil Jordan's film on Michael Collins, even before it appears in the cinemas. Why should not the film itself, and the row concerning it, form a central part of teaching pupils how to evaluate the use of evidence in connection with Collins, and with the War of Independence period? The recent cluster of documentaries on the Great Famine, for instance, could be used to illustrate issues of selection and presentation of material—if only the Great Famine were actually taught to Irish pupils. There is no difficulty in illustrating how the same approach could be adopted in the teaching of languages, or of several other subjects. The teaching of mathematics at second level could be enlivened, indeed should be enlivened, by introducing pupils to the use and abuse of statistical evidence, or even the simplest arithmetical evidence, in public discourse.

This is not a question of teachers instructing pupils in the 'errors' of the media. Rather it is an exploration of the reasons why the media adopts particular perspectives or reaches particular conclusions—why the programmes ask the questions they ask, why they adopt their particular approach. The fundamental question is not whether they are right or wrong, but why have they reached a particular conclusion in the light of the evidence. This will, of course, deepen pupils' understanding of the specific topic under discussion, but more importantly it will equip them with the techniques of thinking which should enable them to evaluate media presentations from an independent perspective throughout their lives. This should constitute a significant part of all curriculum reviews and of all in-service courses for teaching—because teachers themselves need guidance in these matters.

It is preposterous to throw up a wall between the education system and the world outside from which pupils, students, and increasingly teachers, take the bulk of their ideas. However good our education system may be, and much of it is very good, it will never achieve its full potential in educating for citizenship until it acknowledges the crucial role now played by the media in shaping citizens' minds and educates them in the techniques of thinking necessary to evaluate adequately this source of influence on themselves. A vibrant mass media has become a prerequisite for a vibrant mass democracy. But in public discourse, the media ought to exist for the people, not the people for the media. A media orthodoxy cannot be allowed to simply supersede ear-

lier orthodoxies. One orthodoxy succeeding another does not constitute progress. It is simply the opposite side of the same coin. If a breakthrough is to be finally made towards a new Ireland in which genuine
independence of thought can flourish among the populace, and a genuinely pluralistic society emerge, it is essential that a genuinely pluralistic perspective emerge in the media also. Private sector media will
look after its own sectoral interests. It is the unique responsibility of
public sector media to represent the public interest. And that means
ensuring a genuine range of views on contentious issues among public
service broadcasters.

Does public service broadcasting really serve the public?

BOB COLLINS*

The conference programme asks: 'Does the media wish to inform, entertain, or change us?' The Reithian principle of broadcasting (informing, educating, and entertaining), while embodying important standards, is satisfactory only up to a point, because there is an implication in it that audiences are in some way simply passive recipients of what is directed at them, with no ability to respond or adopt a more active posture. I think that we need to re-examine the traditional principles that underlie broadcasting and the ways in which these principles are articulated.

Most people would agree that there is an important role for the media in reflecting the community of which we all form a part, and in reflecting the complexity of that community. That role is not just to hand down established truths. Public broadcasting has a role in reflecting the lives of individuals, in giving people a sense of identity, in exploring the issues that concern people, and in investigating those things that need investigation. In fulfiling these functions it provides detached and objective sources of information to the audience and a window on the wider world. Whether or not the media should change people is something that has been a topic of debate for a considerable time; it is certainly frequently accused of trying to do so, and I think it would be a pity if it didn't succeed, if the experience of viewing and listening (or reading) left one so totally unmoved as not to be in any sense changed. That certainly would raise serious questions about either the media, the viewer (or listener), or perhaps both. The critical question relates to the nature of the change that is wrought, and to the intent and partiality of the broadcaster, because the charge of seeking to change suggests manipulation. Perhaps that touches on one of the crit-

* When this paper was written, the author was Assistant Director-General of RTE.

ical tests of a public broadcasting service: is it detached and objective (though comprehensive), with no 'line' to sell?

The issue of unconscious assumptions and the way they surface is a fact of life. Nobody who works in broadcasting or anywhere else is a 'political eunuch' drained of views simply because he or she comes into broadcasting. The problem of potential bias has been approached in different ways. The practice of having declared positions, and hence balanced panels of journalists, is applied in other countries. In German broadcasting, for example, there is a political and ideological affiliation between journalist and politics, such that changes in government or the political landscape result in concomitant changes in broadcasting personnel. This gives rise to 'Christian Democrat' and 'Liberal Democrat' journalists and presenters who reflect the prevailing orthodoxy. The difficulty with this is that once you compel broadcasters to declare a position, you can't confine this inquisition to what are deemed 'important' issues. For many people there will be many other issues which are just as important as the issues about which we have had referenda in this country. The complex matrix of declared positions would create a working environment that would lend itself to intimidation and serve only to cloud, rather than clarify, issues. We have operated in the tradition (one of many we have taken from our neighbouring island) that an inherent professionalism will enable people to allow open and honest debate, notwithstanding their own personal views. Our view is that good training should enable people to do that.

I think that not to see the powerful, contemporary media as elements which will induce change in people (and, indeed, not to want to use them to effect change) is to have an impoverished view of the media. At the same time, to view these powerful media as agents of change in a particular direction is to ascribe to them a role which they should not have in a democratic society, particularly in the case of publicly owned media. That doesn't mean that every utterance that is broadcast has to be neutral; it does mean, however, that there has to be a healthy forum for the proliferation of points of view, and that there has to be room for the forceful articulation of strong opinions. I think that there is a degree of mixed thinking on the question of objectivity, impartiality, or that ubiquitous word, 'balance'. Balance is not neutrality; the essence of balance is fairness.

You don't need me to identify many of the recent developments which have taken place in broadcasting in Europe, the fruits of which are available to many people on this island. You are also aware of the changes that are taking place in broadcasting within this state, chief of which has been the growth in the number of channels, particularly in television. Television audiences are showing a far greater degree of mobility and flexibility of approach than they have ever done in relation to internationally generated radio. For a very long time, even in the days when RTE Radio was a limited service, the extent to which the audience availed of British radio was limited, even though that service was available throughout the country.

I think that one of the serious difficulties that confronts European broadcasting is the ill-planned nature of the changes which took place in the early to middle 1980s, such that the process of liberalisation or deregulation extended only to the issue of technology and technical capacity. The debate didn't range beyond that to programme content, a consequence of which was a rapid increase in the number of channels with no thought given to or institutional arrangements made about the contents of those channels. Now there is a growing recognition that the developments in the early 1980s were only part of the solution, and that the proliferation of channels would inevitably introduce cheap, imported, 'lowest common denominator' programming. There is a growing concern that the diversity of European cultural expression and a particular sense of European identity will be lost because of the extent to which European channels draw upon a single source of programming, that is to say, the output of the US television and film sectors. There has been within the European Union a number of policies designed to facilitate a greater degree of expression of European culture in the electronic media, but policy here is running after a runaway train, and it is difficult to catch up. This proliferation in broadcasting channels includes a significant growth in multinational satellite channels owned and operated by conglomerates with no community or cultural affinity, whose programmes come, by and large, from boardrooms rather than from communities. The extent to which these channels have impinged on our own lives, as television viewers and citizens in this state, is but a reflection of their impact throughout Europe and other parts of the world.

The question of diversity and integrated ownership, which has already been discussed in this conference in relation to the press, arises also in relation to television. Satellite distributors, owners, and operators do not operate in isolation, but rather in close conjunction with American producers and the owners of libraries of material. This gives them exclusive access to a wide range of products, creating monopolies which deprive other broadcasters of access to material. I wouldn't like to seem a Luddite, but I do believe that technology is not a master but a facilitator, and that we are not inexorably bound to accept everything that technology can offer. We have some capacity to choose in relation to that which is possible. We do so in a wide range of areas, so why shouldn't we do it in relation to broadcasting? There is a real threat to opportunities for self-expression for individual communities and a consequent threat to their cultural identity, a sense of identity which should not be seen in a narrow, chauvinistic way, but in a way which can survive in a sea of extremely vigorous and well-funded competition. Competition is not in itself a bad thing either on an international or national level. There is a real dilemma for people, however, particularly in small communities and countries like ours—an island of five million people, a state of three and a half million—who want to continue to have a broadcasting service which can, with a comprehensive schedule and programmes of quality, address the needs and interests of an Irish audience in the face of cultural patterns which are being determined by multinational sources linked to no community and responsible to no community.

In our present circumstances then, what is the nature of public service broadcasting? What is its role? Does it really serve the public? I believe it does, if for no other reason than that a publicly owned broadcasting service operates without any hint or shade of personal ownership. There are no shareholders except the people who pay their licence fees. There are no owners' interests to be served within the institution, and the only interests genuinely to be served are those of the audience. This may sound high-minded and lofty, and I am not for one moment claiming that RTE is perfect.

I do not mean to say that those who work in public broadcasting are indifferent to their product or their audience. There is, of course, a clear interest on the part of those who have jobs in public broadcasting in keeping their jobs, an interest which is not unusual and not inappropriate. It seems strange that above all other enterprises or endeavours, the provision of good quality employment in broadcasting is to be deprecated, questioned, and undermined, but 'sin scéal eile'. I think that there is also (or at least should be) a genuine responsiveness to the views of the audience. Of course the relationship is not one of 'Tell us what you want and we'll give it to you', any more than it is in areas such as education, but there is a recognition that the audience has rights, and that they share in the process by which a broadcasting environment is developed and a broadcasting service created. That is why RTE is currently engaging in a consultative process with the public. You will have seen advertisements in the newspapers inviting opinions in relation to the nature of our programme services as an input to our process of developing a programme policy, particularly for the next three years. To this end also, a series of public meetings is taking place to provide the public with an opportunity of expressing their views about the service.

There is an inherent tendency within the media to downplay its significance, to under-rate its potential impact. I don't believe the media is going to change the world. I don't believe it will cause people to somersault and do a complete turn around, but I'm under no illusion whatsoever about the influence the media does have. This influence is one reason why the responsibility of people in the media is greater than that of people working in many other areas of public life. I accept this and, like many here, I have for long been drawing attention to the need for media education. We've made a number of efforts (some of which have not been attended by dramatic success), but more is needed. Every child who goes to school spends from 10 to 15 years addressing the question of literary criticism in one way or another, learning to evaluate speech and writing. They start at the age of four and continue until they leave school. Those who go to college continue to learn this, because the whole of third level education consists in learning to evaluate ideas. At the same time, we do not give them the least capacity to evaluate broadcasting, to distinguish between an indifferent programme, a good programme, and a positively bad programme, or to recognise a political message when hit with it.

I would like to discuss briefly three areas of broadcasting in which I think the formation of policy will be very important over the next few years. The first of these is the question of children's broadcasting. I think that children are a key group in the audience, in the sense that they are the sector towards whom broadcasters have greatest responsibility. I think that in the context of a public broadcasting organisation, people (parents in particular) have legitimate expectations which they will want to see reflected in the broadcasting service. It is also an area where there is a sharp distinction between the attitudes and practices of the public broadcaster and those of commercial broadcasters, particularly multinational broadcasters. Children have become very sophisticated viewers and decoders of television. They are entitled to be taken seriously and not to be patronised. Approaches to children's broadcasting have tended to oscillate between two easy options: to leave the area and starve it of attention and resources or, alternatively, to depend increasingly on acquired, animated material, some of which is very good, but some of which is very bad. This is an area that I was glad to see considered in the government's Green Paper on Broadcasting.

The extent to which children's programming is used, not as an end in itself, not as a means of serving a young audience, but as a mechanism through which merchandising campaigns can be built for the sale of all manner of things, is a depressing and a depressingly common feature of contemporary broadcasting, particularly of contemporary satellite broadcasting. For this reason it would be detrimental were children to depend more on external broadcasting than on indigenous broadcasting for their information, education, and entertainment. Very well-funded, attractively packaged, day-long children's series are having an obvious impact, and the kinds of editorial decisions that are made in relation to material broadcast for children are dramatically different in satellite commercial broadcasting from those operating in public-service broadcasting.

I will again confess that RTE is not perfect in this regard, but there are types of material which we have consistently decided not to transmit because they were inappropriate to offer to a young audience in this community. In doing this we make no judgements about other communities and how people determine their own contexts. This is an area in which there is a shared responsibility between broadcaster and parents, and not the exclusive problem of either one or the other.

Parents have a legitimate expectation that, at a particular time of day when their children are likely to view, they won't have to intervene in the pattern of their children's viewing. They are entitled to be able to place some confidence in judgements which are exercised by people who have editorial responsibility. We don't always get it right, but I think we get it right most of the time because we take care, and I believe every other broadcaster in Ireland will adopt the same view. This is an area, however, where commercial pressure, the need to respond to audience shifts, is probably going to have a greater and more immediate impact than in many other areas. When I say it is a shared responsibility, I mean that it falls to parents as well. Parents can't simply assume that, because a careful judgement is being made, the programme which is being transmitted is suitable for their particular child or children. They, too, have to exercise some degree of judgement in relation to what is suitable for their children. Individual choices have to be made because it is impossible to meet the needs of everyone with a single decision taken in an editorial meeting in a broadcasting organisation, wherever it be located. Notwithstanding this, the role of public broadcasting and the philosophy which informs it is clearly manifest in the nature of the programming provided to children.

The 'tabloidisation' of news presentation taking place in the world around us raises similar issues. Can news be presented in an objective, comprehensive way that does not serve a particular 'line' and does not simply follow whatever happens to be available in terms of pictorial images (in the case of television)? If I focus on television sometimes more than on the print media, it is because it is in satellite television broadcasting that the real manifestation of international, commercial forces are evident. I think that the 'CNN-isation' or the 'Sky-isation' of news raises important issues to which we must respond and of which we must take account in the way we relate to our news service.

We can see the changes in the process of the acquisition of licences for independent stations in Britain which have taken place in broadcasting there since the 1990 Broadcasting Act, and the new competitive and commercial environment in which these stations operate. This causes problems for a community like ours in terms of coverage of both Irish and world events. Is it possible to continue to guarantee an Irish perspective, or at least to offer a perspective that isn't coloured by somebody else's self-interest?

I think that the area of sport eloquently demonstrates the divide between public broadcasting and contemporary, commercial broadcasting. We are all aware of the debate taking place about access to sports events, and we are all familiar with the extent to which access to those events is being denied to conventional broadcasters. For the first time sport is being dealt with, not as a manifestation of the cultural life of a people or community, but as a commodity which is exchanged as if it had no cultural relevance whatsoever. On four occasions in the past 12 months, sporting events took place either in Ireland or involving Irish participants which were not available to the Irish audience. Irrespective of whether you care much about, or are happy with, the televising of professional boxing, the two professional boxing matches between Steve Collins and Chris Eubank were the first occasions on which a sporting event took place on this island which was unavailable to the Irish audience. Not even a news crew was permitted inside Millstreet by the sponsors and promoters of this event, who were Sky TV. The Dunhill and Ryder Cups were unavailable to Irish broadcasting, and therefore to the Irish audience, despite the significant role played by an Irish person in the concluding stages of one of those tournaments. The Ireland-US rugby international was another case in point: for the first time ever, a rugby match involving an Irish team was unavailable to us because those rights were taken by Sky.

This raises fundamental questions, not, as I say, about our deprivation relative to anyone else's, but about the way in which important aspects of community life are overnight transformed into commercial commodities which can be withheld at the stroke of a pen on a chequebook from the people from whom they spring. The rights of citizens, as citizens, as members of the community, and as consumers are set at nought. This is an area where public service broadcasting does serve the public because it provides universal, free access at the point of delivery. There is a licence fee, but in terms of 'the point of delivery' it is free. I think these two principles of universality and comprehensiveness of service, which underlie our understanding of broadcasting in Ireland, are also the two areas which are rapidly changing. Henceforward, services will no longer be comprehensive: commercial and audience-size considerations will determine scheduling, and material will increasingly be only available on a pay-as-you-view basis, and not universally. This raises the prospect of other divides in the information society: between those who can and those who can't receive a particular signal because of where they live, or between those who can and those who can't afford to pay extra for a pay-per-view service because of their income. There is a danger that access to community life, or at least to important aspects of community life, will become restricted. If current trends continue, access to other areas of sport and human endeavour will be determined not on the basis of one's belonging to a community, but on the basis of one's bank balance.

Although one could speak of the future in exclusively doom-laden terms because of the real threats that are facing broadcasting in this state, there are also opportunities. There is a much better informed public than there ever was, in terms of how television and radio are put together. There is a potential for access of a kind that there never was in the past. The convergence of the technologies will make possible the development of community-regional television, just as community local radio is not only a possibility, but a reality.

There is an increasing recognition that the making of programmes is not confined to a priesthood inhabiting a centralised temple, but that it is rather an ability open to a wide range of people. I think that the pluralisation of access to the audience through the development of independent producers and the provision of space in the schedules for independent productions has been a significant cultural shift in relation to broadcasting in this state. This might ultimately have been a more rewarding avenue to explore than the pluralisation of means of distribution, by which I mean the development of more television channels.

In the context of all that I have been saying, the challenge facing RTE is to maintain the comprehensive nature of its scheduling, so as to meet the needs of the whole audience (including minority groups), and to maintain that programming at the centre of its schedules rather than to allow it to drift to the periphery. I always said in the years I was director of TV programmes in RTE that the exact same schedule of programmes could be rejuggled to give us a higher audience, but that that wasn't our purpose. Programmes knowingly intended for certain sectors of the audience were placed at the centre of the schedule because they should be available when the audience for which they were intended was able to view, rather than at a time which would be at least unhelpful and at most marginal. That is the challenge facing a public broadcasting service in this state. It is not desirable, therefore, that 64 per cent of RTE's income would come from commercial sources. It is not that there is any direct correlation between sources of income and editorial decisions, but that sort of imbalance is not desirable because if that process continues it doesn't take long before commercial considerations become the dominant forces, and determine, tend to determine, or seek to determine, how editorial decisions are made. I never once, difficult though some people may find this to believe, in the seven and a half years when I was director of TV programmes, had a representation from our salespeople as to what we should do in relation to our schedules. I know there were many views on certain elements of that schedule, but there was never a formal representation or an attempt from the commercial side of the house to influence editorial decision-making. That is not to say that we are unconcerned at audience figures; if we never earned a penny from commercial revenue, we would want our programmes to be available, and to engage as broad a segment of the audience as possible.

Flawed as every human institution is, I think that in this state, there is a good, comprehensive, disinterested, objective programme service. Not everybody will agree with everything we broadcast (at least I hope not). Not everybody will find everything we broadcast to their taste. Not everybody will find their views adequately reflected in what we broadcast, but I believe that everything we do is underpinned by a commitment to the community, and by a notion of service. That will be increasingly difficult to maintain in programme terms because of the changing environment I have described above. It will be increasingly difficult to find access to programming abroad, to events, and to the funding to make the range, quality, and the depth of programming which an Irish audience needs, particularly at a time when there is such a degree of fragmentation and diversification of channels. If we are confronting 150 channels or 500 channels, virtually all of which come from outside, it is all the more necessary that there be the availability of funding and resources to make programmes of real depth and quality about the life of this community.

Have media practitioners a brief to change society?

DAMIEN KIBERD

Let us begin with a small contradiction. The economist Karl Marx once remarked that 'the philosophers merely interpret history, our task is to change it'. But in the very next breath, Marx would of course have stated that, on the basis of his own method of analysing the path of human history, it would not be possible at all for an individual to impose his or her will on society. In other words, ideas do not create history, but history creates ideas.

Journalists like to think of themselves as being among the 'movers and shakers' in modern society. They believe that in a sense they have a mission to improve society, and perhaps to change it. And in some ways they are correct in this belief. For recent Irish political history does suggest that the intervention of various journalists—particularly journalists working in the political arena—has had an important impact on the course of current affairs. But whereas many journalists have been to the fore in seeking to change the political and social landscape of our country, it is by no means clear yet whether the changes that have occurred are a result of that campaigning or are merely a reflection of the changing objective realities confronting ordinary people in our society.

I propose to outline why I believe that it is most dangerous for journalists to embark upon their daily work fired by a belief in their own capacity to alter the course of public events. I will set out my belief that important changes in the political and legal structures in society may result from good journalism. But I would also argue strongly that, on balance, recent trends in Irish journalism are having a detrimental impact on Irish society and impelling it along a course whose destination is by no means clear. To me, no group should set out to change society unless it has a solid base to work from, unless it has thought out and thought through its fundamental or core principles. If you want to alter the legal structures within which society operates, if you want progressively to erode the authority of those forces which in the past have guided society, if you want to dilute or even to destroy the systems of belief which have animated previous generations, then you must have a very clear idea of what you are about. Those who seek to tear down the great institutions of the past should have some kind of alternative to offer. They should have some very clear vision of what they desire to create. For a society does require some form of direction if it is to prosper. And the individual does require some form of personal certainty in his or her daily life. But it seems to me that the iconoclasts of the modern age—many of whom occupy comfortable and highly paid positions within the media—have no particular vision to offer the ordinary citizen. And that when they have completed their work, the individual may confront nothing better than social atomisation in the personal sphere, and the absence of any 'fixed points' within the legal and ethical systems which direct public affairs.

It would seem to me that it is entirely inappropriate for the media industry to set itself up as the dismantler of the past and the creator of a most unspecified future. The entire media industry is beset by a sequence of significant problems. Finding a solution to those problems won't be easy and it will require not just a change of attitude on the part of journalists, but also a willingness on the part of the owners and managers of media companies to invest in beneficial change.

I believe the central problems at present are as follows:

- the predominance of short-term thinking within media companies and the absence of long-term planning;
- the absence of top-class training for journalists and the haphazard nature of recruitment to the profession of journalism;
- the huge competitive pressures in the open Irish marketplace which can, and do, lead to the making of bad editorial judgements, or in some cases the total absence of judgement;
- the secular switch from fact gathering to commentary in large parts of the industry; and
- the abuse of key media platforms for ideological and political purposes.

Aside from these five central problems, which I believe have led to quite startling imperfections in the media industry here in recent times, there are other key issues that have not been dealt with satisfactorily either by the journalists (individually or collectively) or by the managements of media companies. These include:

- the need to determine what human rights are basic and fundamental, and to achieve in Irish journalism a balance between competing rights;
- the need to determine what is correctly public information and what is correctly private information;
- whether or not journalism should proceed from a presumption of innocence;
- why, even in a highly competitive market, journalists must be absolutely honest with the consumers who pay for the information which they produce;
- why journalists must from time to time cease acting as mere spectators or observers of events and actually make important moral and ethical decisions in relation to the conduct of their own work.

I believe that it is precisely because these issues remain largely unaddressed and because the central problems afflicting the media industry remain untackled, that it is highly dangerous for journalists to see themselves as being on a mission to change society.

Good journalists must operate simultaneously within both a legal and ethical framework. In some cases a journalist will be tempted to ignore both legal and ethical issues. Mostly, however, ethics go on the back burner while the parameters of what is presented to the consumer are determined by legal pressures. Frequently editors and journalists do not ask themselves if what they are doing is ethically correct. They ask themselves if what they propose to publish will be legally actionable, and occasionally they take professional advice from lawyers. But in an industry where circulation and readership figures and audience ratings are the totem poles of achievement, they seldom take time out to reflect on the nature of their work and the need to operate according to sound ethical principles. By failing to engage in constant and ruthless self-analysis, Irish journalists are weakening each day the thread of trust linking them and their work to the wider public.

Some of those who have devoted enormous amounts of time to this subject do not believe that it is possible to teach a journalist or an editor about ethics. Ethics can only be learned and not taught, they say. And the recent history of Irish journalism should have taught us all many important lessons. I made a resolution earlier this year that I would no longer engage in the well known journalistic sport of bashing competing newspapers and media companies. And so in averting to a number of practical case studies which I believe illustrate some of the dangers involved in crusading or campaigning journalism, I will try to be as uncritical as possible of the persons involved and hopefully I can confine myself merely to raising some awkward questions.

None of us is perfect. Some time ago at the *Sunday Business Post* I took a gravely wrong editorial decision. I decided to publish a transcript of three illegally intercepted telephone conversations between the present Taoiseach and three of his senior colleagues. In doing so I was very wrong. I thought at the time that it was a 'good story' and of course it was a highly entertaining one. For the subject of the three conversations was telephone tapping itself. Clearly the story would boost the circulation of my newspaper. But the decision to publish was both illegal and unethical. For the former, I was tried and convicted in the District Court. For the latter I received no punishment at all.

To move on to other practical questions: If a man who is HIV positive comes to you and tells you that he intends to commit suicide and wants you to take down and publish his thoughts on why he has reached such a desperate state, do you agree to his request, or do you tell him that you do not intend to give him any publicity and instead compel him to seek psychiatric help? If a broken-down chartered accountant comes to you and tells you that he has been uttering forged letters, the purpose of which is to spread poison about certain individuals, should you give him the platform of a half hour of current affairs television, liberally laced with innuendo? Should a newspaper editor later have the same self-confessed liar wired-up with listening devices in a bid to entrap a series of business people by engaging them in conversation on the telephone? If a well known pop star has an affair with the governess of his children, should you send photographers to take pictures of those children at their school? Should you allow reporters to pursue the wife of the pop star who has already been deeply hurt by his actions? What public interest is served by such behaviour on the part of reporters and photographers?

If a politician is spoken to by the police at night in an area where gay men consort, is the public interest served by bringing this fact to light, even if the work of that politician has no bearing on the nature of his social life? Does the right of that man and his family to retain a sense of human dignity exceed the alleged right of the public to acquire knowledge of his actions?

If a bishop is unmasked as a thoroughgoing hypocrite and is shown to have been involved in a prolonged affair and to have fathered a son, and if he further uses diocesan funds, at least temporarily, to deal with his problems, then clearly it is both in the public interest and ethically proper that these facts should be brought to light by the media. But at what point does an editor decide that the public interest has been sufficiently served by the publication of relevant facts, and that further coverage of the matter would amount to little more than voyeurism which would probably have the effect of stripping away the right to human dignity of those involved? Or, to put it more practically, should the woman involved in the relationship be encouraged to go on publicly funded radio to describe the most private details of that relationship and to express moral judgements on her former partner?

These are some of the questions that force journalists and editors to learn about ethics in the course of their daily work. But without being too judgmental myself, I think it is fair to say that many bad decisions have been taken in the recent past by journalists and editors. These decisions have been taken and these judgements made in the heat of the moment and without proper reflection. The mistakes flow, I believe, from the fundamental failure to address basic problems and issues within the media industry.

In a recent article, the columnist Fintan O'Toole said that what has happened in recent decades is akin to the work of a farmer in clearing rocks from a very stony field. The media has been to the fore in pushing a new secular agenda, which has resulted in rock after rock being taken from the field, sometimes only after a false start. Clearly, much of the work of removing the rocks contains great merit. A great deal of what was rotten and hypocritical has been destroyed. But so much energy has been expended in clearing the field of rocks and circumstances have changed so much in the meantime that when the field is finally cleared, nobody knows what crop to plant in it. O'Toole's analogy is a telling one. For many of those who have spearheaded the drive to clear the various rocks from the field no longer have any clear vision of what they intended to create. Whereas in the late sixties and the seventies many of those seeking change wanted to create a socialist society, following the collapse of the centrally planned economies, they too have been robbed of their basic philosophy. And society does need some form of vision or philosophy as a sort of glue that can serve to bind the disparate elements.

But there is no basic philosophy evident among those who have helped to forge the current political consensus, a consensus which means that all six major political parties are likely to agree on a wide range of issues. And worse still, those who do not share the thinking of the politically correct classes are in danger of being marginalised and even disenfranchised. For example, during the referendum on divorce some 49.7 per cent of voters opposed the legalisation of divorce. Yet with the exception of a rather stormy debate at the Fianna Fáil Ard Fheis, the political preferences of such people were more or less ignored by the political elite. Those few journalists who expressed genuine fears about the creation of a divorce culture were cold-shouldered by their colleagues in the media.

Could I pose a question at this stage? Who will accept responsibility for the likely future consequences of present actions that are being sold to the public by journalists and commentators on the basis that they represent a worthy extension of personal freedoms or the creation of a new set of human or civil rights?

During the divorce referendum it was obvious that at the beginning of the campaign many important parts of the media were determined to present the arguments in a balanced fashion. But as the support for a 'no' vote began to increase in the opinion polls, objectivity went out the window and newspapers became nakedly partisan. The use of loaded language featured in what purported to be objective news reports. The media succeeded in helping the political establishment out of a tight corner in this instance. But what will the response of the media be if in years to come it turns out that the worst fears of the anti-divorce campaigners are realised—if, for example, one third of Irish marriages collapse, leading to huge financial pressures on both individuals and the state? It seems to me that the process upon which the media wishes society to embark is a one-way street. Just as there is no going back, there is hardly going to be any critical analysis of that process either as it unfolds. And how ethical is it for a cadre of well-paid and privileged individuals within the media industry to press so relentlessly for change, and in such an uncritical fashion, if they cannot be certain of the consequences of their actions and if they have no solutions to offer to the problems which may flow from their deeds?

In all of this opinion forming, one rather obvious problem springs to mind. While it may prove relatively straightforward to construct a system of ethics governing the reporting of established facts, no system of ethics that might apply to the expression of opinions by journalists yet exists. The world of opinion is a whole lot bigger than the world of fact, so the problem of creating a system of ethics for this area is going to prove to be very, very difficult. And there is a welter of opinion expressed each day in our national newspapers. Some of our most successful media products actually employ partisan commentary as a feature of their front pages. The *Sunday Independent* is a case in point. In recent weeks when the newspaper had commissioned a thoroughly professional survey of public attitudes to the peace process, instead of leading the front page with details of the statistical findings of the survey it instead employed an academic based at University College, Cork, to put a personal gloss on the results.

I have worked as a journalist for 17 years. One thing I have found most remarkable about the world of Dublin journalism is the relative absence of internal debate. Journalists tend to travel in packs. Like the peloton following the man in the yellow jersey during the Tour de France, the corps of journalists based at RTE and within the national newspapers tends to adopt uniform opinions upon the issues of the day. As the necessity to research facts by contacting members of the wider public evaporates, and as the vogue for commentary increases, the possibility that the peloton might be wholly out of touch with public opinion can at times reach dangerous proportions. Because journalists like nothing better than to socialise with one another in the capital's restaurants and bars, and because they are constantly mixing with people from similar social backgrounds, they may be fully convinced of the 'correctness' of certain ideas and may embrace what might be termed as a 'conventional wisdom'. And when the columns of newspapers are in turn dominated by the most strident and assertive forms of social commentary, it is perfectly possible that journalists may embark upon a crusade on behalf of ideas and proposals which find little or no support in the wider community. Therein lies the danger that a so-called cognitive elite may seek to alter society from above in a manner which is entirely unwelcome to a vast group in society.

To put it plainly: instead of talking to ordinary people, many journalists may actually spend a large part of the day talking to each other. The net result is that the mass media are no longer a locus of true debate but instead become a focus for rather partisan campaigning. I think that the truth of what I am saying has been recognised in the recent past, even by those forces controlling the mainstream media. In an important contribution to this ongoing debate, for example, the editor of the *Irish Times*, Conor Brady, recently stated that he regretted that there was no national newspaper group in this country that might offer a countervailing view to what has become the media orthodoxy. He explained, and I would accept, that his own newspaper had a specific vision of what it wished to support and of the sort of society it desired.

But is there a solution to this problem? The creation of new newspapers is by no means a simple task. Aside from the obvious difficulty of fashioning a newspaper which appeals to a commercially viable audience, huge amounts of capital are required if a newspaper is to be in true control of its destiny. And it is not just capital for investment in good journalism and in marketing, it is capital for investment in buildings and in printing machines. It is not easy to convince those with capital to apply it to the creation of a better balance within the media industry, in a country where newspapers are already under severe financial pressures and where the problems posed by a domestic near-monopoly are compounded by the openness of the local economy to a flood of imported products.

The peace process: who defines the news—the media or government press offices?

BRIAN FEENEY

What I tell you three times is true. 'When I use a word,' Humpty Dumpty said in a rather scornful tone, 'it means just what I choose it to mean—neither more nor less.'

Even though the concept of 'primary definition' wasn't invented until about 20 years ago, Lewis Carroll evidently knew about it when he was writing *Alice in Wonderland* and *The Hunting of the Snark*. In *Policing the Crisis* published in 1978, Professor Stuart Hall and his co-authors claimed governments were able to define the issues at stake whenever the media became interested in an event or topic. The media, then, does not simply 'create' the news; nor does it simply transmit the ideology of the 'ruling class' in a conspiratorial fashion. Indeed, we have suggested that, in a critical sense, the media is frequently not the 'primary definers' of news events at all; but their structured relationship to power has the effect of making it play a crucial but secondary role in reproducing the definitions of those who have privileged access, as of right, to the media as 'accredited sources'. From this point of view, in the moment of news production, the media stands in a position of structured subordination to the primary definers.[1]

To put it simply, when the media thinks it is accurately reporting a story, what it is often doing is retailing a version of the truth provided by official sources. It can't not report what official sources tell it, and although it may be sceptical, often there is no time to check it out or go to another source to obtain balance. Often the timing of the announcement is deliberately such that there is no time for journalists in the electronic media to find an alternative view. The people timing the

1 S. Hall, C. Crichter, T. Jefferson, J. Clarke, and B. Roberts, *Policing the Crisis: Mugging, the State and Law and Order* (London, 1978), p.59.

announcement also take advantage of the competition in the media to be first.

What I want to explore here is the competition to define issues and topics about the peace process in the past six months. It is an enormous area. To give it a full treatment would require examination of newspapers, tabloid and broadsheet, both here and in Britain and the United States, hundreds of radio broadcasts, and television news and current affairs programmes on a variety of channels both terrestrial and satellite. Given the constraints of time and resources, I intend to stick mainly to the coverage by terrestrial TV in Ireland and Britain. This is how the majority of people first hear about events. I will look at three critical events and try to analyse how governments tried to 'define' them, which government 'won' and what conclusions can be drawn.

First a few observations about coverage of Northern Ireland. This contribution to the seminar was originally to be called 'Whose news is it anyway?—Can there be a national news bulletin when the audience doesn't belong to the nation?' My thinking on this was justified when I was advised that few people in the Republic would understand that title. Let me try to explain what I mean. Virtually all European states have national TV and radio, or one station which is pre-eminently the official, or quasi-official channel. In these islands the stations are RTE and BBC1. Both stations would probably resist such a description, and certainly journalists working for those channels would deny the description. But politicians and governments have expectations of TV and radio different from journalists and producers. They like them to broadcast their view of the world exclusively. For example, last August the Romanian Government banned state television from broadcasting BBC news in Romanian. BBC news might be critical of Romania's human rights record towards its minorities. It wouldn't do if the BBC said anything that encouraged the two million Hungarians trapped in Romania by the border drawn in 1923. Politicians expect national TV to create a national identity, and they know that happens not only because of news bulletins. Soaps are just as important. They are the topic of conversation everywhere each day. There have been critical moments in the fictional lives of soap stars which have almost brought countries to a standstill. The departure of Bette Lynch in 'Coronation Street' is one recent example. In this sense TV can collapse class distinctions. Everyone has a common reference point, an item to discuss, a shared reference point and a view to contribute, even if it's only irritation. It is so pervasive that tabloid newspapers devote acres of space to the characters in soaps.

But it's more than this. David Miller, in his authoritative study of the media and the North, says the BBC is 'expected to foster a consensual national identity'.[2] It doesn't always and often voices critical of the official line are heard. But life is made difficult for them. Enormous pressure has been exerted to prevent certain programmes being broadcast. 'At the Edge of the Union', depicting Sinn Féin's Martin McGuinness and Gregory Campbell of the DUP in Derry, is probably the best known example in recent years. Similar pressure has been exerted on RTE, not only through the most obvious means of Section 31. RTE had to submit rather more quickly than the BBC because its relationship with government is much tighter.

But the most important point for the purposes of this paper is that both the BBC and ITN, on the one hand, and RTE, on the other, are watched by a large audience which is not formally part of the 'national consensus' in either Britain or Ireland. Quite simply, millions of people in Ireland watch British TV and many are more likely to see 'News at Ten' on ITN than the 'Nine O'Clock News' on RTE. Similarly, many people in the Republic see 'UTV Live', and ten of thousands in the North watch RTE news and programmes like 'Primetime'. In other words, 'national' news bulletins and current affairs programmes are often watched by an audience in the North that rejects the interpretation placed on the information it receives, and by an audience in the South which often unwittingly takes in the British spin on events because they have no first-hand information available to counter it. Probably more people get their information from Irish editions of British newspapers and British TV (and I include BBCNI and UTV in this definition) than from Irish media outlets. Ireland's position must be unique in this respect in that the television viewers are exposed to the attempts at primary definition by another country's government.

This is not to suggest that the British Government tries to define issues and topics for an Irish audience. In case people may think I have

---

2 David Miller, *Don't Mention the War: Northern Ireland, Propaganda, and the Media* (London, 1994).

either an inflated idea of the importance of Ireland for the British Government, or some degree of paranoia, let it be clear that the efforts of the British Government are not confined to Irish news items. On the contrary, the evidence seems to be the British Government pays no attention at all to Irish viewers and listeners: and that is part of the problem. The effort is to create the desired impression in its own elec-torate. The British Government goes to great lengths to 'define' topics in its own favour. It has to do this because much of TV, and increasing-ly the press, is critical of this government. Just look at the preparations by the British Government to ensure it controlled the definition of issues dealt with by the Scott Report into arms sales to Iraq.

Here is an example of the scale of the effort. In 1994-95 the Home Office spent £42,000 per working day promoting itself in the media—that is four times the cost of the Home Office's entire staff and running costs in Whitehall.[3] However, it pales into insignificance beside the NIO's (Northern Ireland Office) efforts. In the fiscal year 1989-90, the NIO spent £20 million on PR work and information.[4] The Northern Ireland Information Service, the press division of the NIO, delivers three packets of press releases every day: that could amount to a dozen separate items. In 1992 it had a staff of 58 in Belfast and London. In 1990 it spent £7.2 million in the North alone for a population of 1.5 million, compared to £1.4 million by the Scottish Office for a population of five million. But the NIO also peppers for-eign embassies and press agencies with NIO releases. The police and (before 1994) the British Army also deploy vast PR resources which mount up to the total of about £20 million. The PR empire of the NIO is spun by Andy Wood, a former deputy of Sir Bernard Ingham at Downing Street. He is a vastly experienced professional operator with unrivalled experience in the corridors of Whitehall and matchless con-tacts in British government. Everyone has heard of Seán Duignan and Shane Kenny. Andy Wood remains in the shadows.

The peace process, however, changed the balance of power in both the Irish and British governments. Until 1994 the NIO and the Department of Foreign Affairs ran the North and the Secretary of State for Northern Ireland and the Tánaiste for the Republic led for

3 £10.9 million on the media and £2.6 million other (Hansard).
4 Much of what follows is taken from Miller (1994), appendices B and C.

the two governments. When peace appeared an attainable aim in 1994, for some reason the Taoiseach's Office and the Cabinet Office in Whitehall muscled in on the action. This had a number of consequences for media management.

Firstly, on the English side, instead of one department, the NIO, handling everything, Whitehall took over, and although the NIO was quickly relegated to the second division, nevertheless different emphases have come from the two sources. On the Irish side the Tánaiste was less ready to yield ground, partly because he is a party leader in his own right but also because officials in Foreign Affairs had been running Northern policy for decades, while no one in the Taoiseach's Office had any experience (apart from Martin Mansergh and he left with Fianna Fáil three months after the ceasefire). Secondly, in spring 1995 the Department of Justice was brought in to examine decommissioning of weapons. The department secretary, Mr Dalton, began a series of meetings with the permanent secretary at the NIO, Sir John Chilcott. So now three departments of the Irish Government were involved.

While all these departmental arrangements might seem a bit tedious, their importance for the argument being presented here is that the Irish press presentation became more diffuse while the British line became a single, clear one. Increasingly it came from the Cabinet Office alone. In Ireland journalists could go to three departments and obtain a different view of what was important from each. Obviously if all the Department of Justice was working on was decommissioning, that would assume greater importance for that department than say, for Foreign Affairs. But on top of three departments involved in Dublin there was the added complication of a coalition government. The Irish cabinet committee on the North is essentially the leaders of the three coalition parties who have in the past held widely divergent views about the North. Now while officials have to be very circumspect about what they say to the press, party leaders who are government ministers can give their own views. On a series of issues strains have been evident among the three. The British have been accused of trying to insert a wedge between the Taoiseach (John Bruton) and the Tánaiste (Dick Spring), but a substantial wedge already separated the Minister for Social Welfare (Proinsias de Rossa) and the Tánaiste.

So what effect has this proliferation of departmental responsibility and political involvement had on the media's coverage of the peace process? The British have benefited from the division of labour on the Irish side. The NIO likes to present an image of a unified department with one mind; the same goes for the British Cabinet Office. It is far from the truth. The security advice to the NIO repeatedly rejected the demand for decommissioning which came from London. The RUC Chief Constable reiterated on a number of occasions that it was meaningless. The fact that he did so indicates his concern about the consequences of insisting on this political demand. But no politician in the NIO publicly or privately backed the chief constable's view.

Once the media has detected differences it exploits them and it is usually impossible to plaster over the cracks. The paradox is that before the ceasefire it was easier to detect differences among the British, whereas afterwards it has become easier to detect differences among the Irish. Take the British side first. Before the ceasefire there were obvious divisions about security policy. The best known was the competition among the RUC, MI5, and the British Army. In 1992, confidential minutes of a Metropolitan Police meeting were leaked to the *Irish Times* and subsequently printed in British newspapers. The leak was designed to help MI5.

The minutes showed the Met had 'little hard intelligence' on IRA personnel in Britain. The leak occurred in the middle of a ferocious tussle for control of operations against the IRA. Shortly afterwards, MI5 took charge of the anti-IRA role of the Special Branch. Without such tensions it is easier to maintain the image of unity. Furthermore, political control has passed completely to John Major who presides over a united cabinet sub-committee on Ireland. Sir Patrick Mayhew, the Secretary of State, is an utterly loyal supporter of Major and depends completely on the Prime Minister for his position in the cabinet; at 67 he is one of its oldest members. The others, Michael Howard, Michael Portillo, Michael Heseltine (it obviously helps to be called Michael), Lord Cranborne, Malcolm Rifkind, and Brian Mawhinney, have no alternative policies on Ireland to pursue. In fact, Ireland is incidental to their portfolios. Any decision the sub-committee takes on Ireland will be rapidly executed by the Cabinet Office.

There will be no leaks because no one is pursuing a rival policy line and therefore no advantage can accrue to any member by a leak.[5]

On the Irish side, given the natural differences on the North among the three coalition parties, the government has performed extremely well. However, it has been handicapped both in formulating policy and in responding to British proposals by the necessity for the three leaders to meet as a committee before they produce an agreed position. The fact that they do produce an agreed position is a tribute to their will to keep the government together, but the process causes delay. The British have been aware of this delayed reaction and used it to their own advantage. But they have also taken the initiative on occasions and successfully managed the media to define their position as the correct or dominant one. They have done this when they decided they could not agree with the Irish position. The British took their decision, went to the media to present it there first, and on each such occasion the Irish Government has been left flat-footed. The decommissioning issue is the best example. The Irish Government has been at sixes and sevens about how to respond since it first arose in Spring 1995.

I will look at three instances of media management in detail: first the aborted summit scheduled for 6 September 1995; second the summit meeting on 28 November 1995; and, finally, the launch of the Mitchell Report on 24 January 1996.

The aborted summit

There was to be a summit on 6 September 1995. That was a Wednesday. The Irish Government agonised over the previous week-end and decided finally and reluctantly on Tuesday 5 September they could not proceed. They told the British by lunch time and then for some reason did nothing. No position was prepared. The British realised an explanation would be needed for the failure of the Taoiseach and Prime Minister to meet next day. They decided quickly to get their explanation in first. They rapidly organised briefings and

---

5 The last major leak from the British side was the Framework Document. It almost certainly came from this sub-committee and was designed to help Unionists. The nature of the leak indicates the right-wing bias of the sub-committee and reinforces the view that the members have been satisfied with the slow progress and lack of concessions to Republicans over the 17 months of the ceasefire.

interviews. Sir Patrick Mayhew appeared live on the the BBC 'Nine O'Clock News' and 'Newsnight'. Michael Brunson, a reliable barometer of the British Government line on 'foreign' affairs, had been given a ferocious briefing about the Irish Government, which he duly delivered at full volume to Trevor MacDonald on 'News at Ten'. The message was simple. It was the Irish Government who had 'lost their bottle' and given in to Sinn Féin. The message was for the British people and they got it. The British Government won hands down on Tuesday night. The Irish Government was left at the post. The British also carried all the English newspapers with their line on Wednesday, except *The Independent*.

But of course nationalists in the North, and a sizeable slew of people in the Republic, watched the same news. When the northerners see someone like Mayhew, who is a poor TV performer, 'making himself available', as the phrase goes, live, they know a snow job is under way. Because there are two communities watching the same news which transmits a message designed for Britain, the result is to increase division in the North. Unionists bought the story and accused the Irish Government of cowardice solely on the basis of what they heard from the British media. But nationalists knew that if the British were trying so hard there must be another story. They instinctively backed the Irish Government. So they turned to RTE, but in vain: one nil to Britain there too.

It wasn't until 24 hours later that the Irish Government caught up. But they were on the back foot, having to deny the British line. Now while you couldn't expect the BBC and ITN not to take their own government's line against the Irish Government, you could expect the Irish Government press office to have a line prepared to counter the British attack. You could also expect the Irish Government to wonder how the story would play in the North, given that the two communities have different perceptions about every political move.

The Irish Government also failed to capitalise on how nervous the British Government was about how the United States administration would receive the news of the collapse of the planned summit. Their nervousness was one of the reasons for the vehement attack on the Irish position. The evidence for this is that on Wednesday night Admiral Crowe, the US ambassador to London, arrived in Downing Street, called in by John Major, according to British sources, to explain Britain's position; to express President Clinton's concern at the collapse of the summit, Irish and American sources said. On Thursday, Michael Ancram dropped everything and flew to Washington. BBCNI was now talking about Ancram giving 'the British version' of what happened. But while keen observers knew Oscar Wilde's epigram, 'the truth is rarely pure and never simple', was being ratified again, the majority of people only knew the British position.

The November summit

The second occasion when wide differences between the two governments were exposed was just before President Clinton's visit in November/December 1995. In the run up to this visit intensive efforts were made by officials of both the British and Irish governments and the US Government to cobble something together that would enable President Clinton to claim progress in Ireland. The issue had crystallised around the British and Unionist demand for decommissioning of weapons first and the Irish and Northern nationalist demand for all-party talks first. That had ruined the September summit and no agreement could be reached to square the circle. Finally the two governments were able to arrange a summit on 28 November, in which it was agreed that former Senator Mitchell would examine the issue of decommissioning. There was a great deal of toing and froing over the weekend of 24-26 November during which the NIO in London and the Cabinet Office briefed the English press to the effect that agreement could have been reached, and indeed nearly had been reached until officials from the Department of Foreign Affairs had arrived in London on Saturday 25 November. It looked as if there was going to be an action replay of 6 September when the British successfully defined the issue as being the Irish Government's readiness to accommodate Sinn Féin and unwillingness to require them to make hard decisions. At all costs the British were determined to portray themselves to the Americans as the injured party and the Irish as the intransigent one.

Furthermore, extensive briefings indicated that while the officials in the Taoiseach's Office were more amenable and had more or less reached an agreement with their counterparts in the British Cabinet

Office on the night of Friday 24 November, certain officials in Foreign Affairs, whom they named, had overturned this agreement on 25 November. This sounded exactly the same as the briefing of 5 September, namely, 'We thought we had an agreement, but the rats got at it.' This line continued through Monday 27 November with Robin Oakley, the BBC's political editor, reporting on the 'Nine O'Clock News' that 'the atmosphere is deteriorating'. He blamed Foreign Affairs and the Department of Justice and said there was 'ill feeling and accusations'. He concluded that, 'London hopes Clinton will pressure Adams. London is confident Clinton is behind them.' This was a clear British attempt at 'definition' for the benefit of a British audience. In fact, Washington was exerting pressure on London where the NIO and the Cabinet Office were unmoving on decommissioning. But the arguments had gone on for too many days for the British Government's attempt at definition to succeed. On ITN's 'News at Ten' on 27 November, Michael Brunson retailed the simplistic pro-government line. But former US Congressman Bruce Morrison was also interviewed. He said, 'Everyone has moved but Britain in the last five months.' On BBC2 'Newsnight' there was a balanced discussion with contributions from London, Dublin, and Washington, featuring Proinsias De Rossa, Michael Mates MP, and Bruce Morrison. The British Government line was not sustained in the media.

But it is interesting to note that the most severe questioning of that line came from the BBC. Indeed, the BBC actually devoted more time to the issue than RTE. The report on the BBC's 'Nine O'Clock News' on 27 November lasted seven minutes compared to five on RTE. While the British media broadcast its government's attempts to blame the Irish, RTE reported that the impasse that day had ended hopes for a summit meeting before Clinton's visit. RTE then moved on to the divorce referendum.

When, to everyone's surprise a summit occurred late on the night of 28 November, huge resources were deployed by each government to take credit for what had happened. On RTE's 'Nine O'Clock News' it was claimed it had all been sparked by the Taoiseach's speech to the Meath Association in London a fortnight before. There was a long background piece with an obvious Foreign Affairs spin. British television coverage relegated the issue because it was Budget Day. BBC

'Nine O'Clock News' understandably devoted 18 minutes to the budget and four minutes to the summit breakthrough. But the late-night arrival of the Irish Government delegation in London for the joint press conference to launch the summit communiqué was so dramatic that the British media carried it on 29 November alongside the budget details.

In this instance the process of trying to claim credit, or at least the high ground, began in the middle of November with a letter from John Major to John Bruton making various 'proposals'. In other words, the British portraying themselves as the people who took the initiative. John Bruton replied with a letter of his own before 24 November. The conclusion must be that the prolonged posturing from the middle of the month, which progressed to intensive negotiations from 24 November through to the summit and the Clinton visit on 30 November, and the obvious efforts by both governments to take credit for the meeting and the contents of the communiqué made it clear to the media that it was the Americans who had forced the pace. American spin doctors with the president were also trying to define their government's role. The media therefore did not buy either the British or the Irish government's line in toto. But at least in this instance the Irish Government was fully engaged and did have a line to present.

The Mitchell Report

The final occasion I want to deal with is the presentation of the Mitchell Report on 24 January 1996. The two governments had received it on 22 January and the Irish Government strove to establish a common response with the British. It is clear now that the British Government had decided by 23 January that it could not accept Mitchell's proposal to go straight to all-party talks with decommissioning happening alongside. Regardless of what John Major told John Bruton on the telephone that night, the British Government had prepared a media onslaught to carry its view on 24 January. The general consensus is that the Irish Government was 'mugged'. After Major's announcement of elections in the House of Commons, he then went to a pre-arranged series of interviews. Robin Oakley interviewed him on BBC 'Six O'Clock News'. The item lasted 11 minutes. Major also gave interviews to Channel 4, ITN, and BBC2 'Newsnight'. He had obviously cleared his diary for this the day before, in the full knowledge of the level of controversy his announcement was going to provoke. All the British media outlets initially accepted that Major's proposal for an election was reasonable and democratic. Why would they not? It was completely supported by the Labour Party and the House of Commons as a whole. Party leaders had all received briefings. Only John Hume and the Irish Government had not. Michael Brunson on 'News at Ten' said, 'For some reason John Hume felt it necessary to voice his suspicions.' Hume's was the only voice of disagreement because the Irish Government said nothing for hours.

It was a brilliant ambush by the British. John Bruton was flying off to Strasbourg in the afternoon. RTE carried Major's response to the Mitchell report on Aertel, its teletext news, for most of the afternoon. There was nothing about the Irish Government's position on BBC or RTE for hours because there wasn't a position. John Bruton appeared on RTE 'Six-One' news in an interview with Eamon Lawlor pre-recorded while Major was speaking. Channel 4 news at 7 pm carried a clip from that interview in which they said the Taoiseach agreed with Major's idea! Bruton appeared on ITN at 10.00 pm interviewed in the street in Strasbourg. He was floundering. The first clear response was Dick Spring's on 'Primetime' at the special time of 8.30 pm. It became known that the Irish Government found out about Major's line less than an hour before he spoke. British channels devoted one hour and 20 minutes to the issue whereas RTE's coverage was less than an hour. The British had defined the issue as a democratic opportunity to test opinion. Everyone kept asking Irish ministers why they objected to an election. This was a classic example of primary definition. The British had devised a strategy and planned the media tactics to carry it off. But curiously in a number of such cases RTE doesn't seem to realise there's a contest. It even initially buys the British definition. It happened on 6 September 1995 and again on 24 January 1996. I am not alone in this observation. Northern nationalists are often astonished at the accep-tance by RTE of the British line. But this is the view of the *Irish Times* television critic, Eddie Holt, on 27 January.

It's hard to work out what RTE's 'Nine O'Clock News' on Wednesday [24 January] was thinking of with a (second) headline that said: 'John Major says he's ready to introduce legislation to allow for

Northern elections, but the parties remain divided. . .' Perhaps it is just me, but the thrust and tone of that headline either misses or—worse—deliberately obscures the whole spirit of Major's reaction to the Mitchell Report. As this RTE headline told it, John Major was being positive and magnanimous in his response to the report. Good man John!

The phrase, 'says he's ready to introduce legislation to allow for Northern elections', suggests a move on John Major's part which might not be in his own interests and, indeed, might even be motivated by altruism. Naturally, this is how John Major would wish his readiness 'to introduce legislation' to be seen. But, clearly, that was not the case. So what was going on? Did editors and journalists in RTE believe John Major's response to be positive and magnanimous? On the Wednesday, the RTE news fell—either wittingly or unwittingly—for propaganda even cruder than you would expect from 'Murder One'. But all the blame cannot be assigned to RTE. If there is no guidance coming from its own government what should it do? Devise its own definition and perhaps receive an exocet from Iveagh House? Maybe the Irish Government agrees with the British definition? After all are they not supposed to be acting jointly? In the words of Professor Hall, RTE often finds itself 'in a position of structured subordination to the primary definers'; and in most cases in the last six months the primary definers were the British Government.

It seldom works the other way. What is an issue of national importance in Ireland often never sees the light of day in England. For example, in December 1995 the Irish Government was mightily exercised by the fate of Irish Steel at Cork. There was a prospect that the British Government might veto a subsidy from Europe to the plant. In Ireland acres of newsprint and aeons of air time were lavished on the issue. There was scarcely a mention in the British media. Admittedly it coincided with a fisheries dispute in England, but the British attitude to Irish Steel placed a Major-Bruton summit on 21 December in jeopardy. It got one clause on BBC 'Breakfast Time' that day. It was reported that the summit had a question mark over it because of a 'dispute between the two countries over a steel plant'. To an English viewer it would have seemed an inexplicably minor issue to cause a hiccough between the two premiers. Of course they were not told it was the only

such plant in Ireland. Yet there were fears in the nationalist community in the North that Bruton would do a deal: a subsidy for Irish Steel in
return for a Northern Assembly. It may seem far fetched but the suspicions in the North were real. *An Phoblacht/Republican News* ran extensive stories on Irish Steel throughout December. None of that ever sur-
faced in England.

You would be entitled to believe the royal visits to Ireland on 19/20
January would attract British attention. Princess Anne and Prince
Edward carried out a large number of engagements ranging from the
West to Dublin. There were joint engagements with President
Robinson. There was massive coverage in the Irish media and the visits
were regarded as a major gesture of reconciliation. British press and
TV virtually ignored the events. Similarly, visits by President Robinson
to Africa, which were given the full treatment by RTE, receive no time
in Britain. For example, the president's visit to Rwanda in early
October was ignored. On 4/5 January it was announced that President
Robinson would engage in an official visit to England that year. Again
RTE treated this as a major advance in relations between the two countries. BBC and ITN didn't carry it.

But it is not impossible to achieve a hearing on the British media.
When the Irish counter-proposals to Major's election plans finally
emerged on 7 February the Irish Government did a good job. The
announcement of the proposal for proximity talks came as northern
Britain was suffering the worst blizzards for 50 years. Even so, BBC
'Six O'Clock News' placed the Irish initiative second after a report that
the Scott inquiry would be released on 15 February. John Bruton gave
an interview on BBC 'Nine O'Clock News' and he appeared live on
BBC2 'Newsnight' where Dick Spring gave a recorded interview. The
proposals were given a fair hearing. Strangely, on RTE the item came
third after the rejection of the Hanafin divorce appeal and an item on
rural murders.

The good coverage on 7 February 1996 was obviously the result of
hard work and preparation. The evidence suggests there is no inherent
hostility to a case the Irish Government might put. For example, after
the uproar that followed Major's election announcement, British TV
examined the issue in detail and mounted some trenchant criticism. On
25 January, the day after the Mitchell Report, 'Newsnight' ran a story

on it during which there was a three-way interview with Niall O'Dowd, editor of the *Irish Voice*, and Andrew Hunter MP, chairman of the Conservative backbench committee on Northern Ireland. O'Dowd comprehensively defeated Hunter. The British Government line did not hold. But it was too late. Major's proposals had gained a fair wind in the press as well as on television. Apart from the careful planning of the ambush, another technique helped. It is called a 'hierarchy of access'. The NIO has been operating this procedure for many years. Quite simply it is this: the NIO offers different levels of facilities to different audiences depending on the agenda it wants to advance. Their main audience is the British public followed closely by the United States. At the bottom comes the Republic. Accordingly, there is almost no chance of an Irish journalist getting an interview with John Major or Sir Patrick Mayhew except in the most controlled circumstances and in any case not live.

The NIO has no interest in public opinion in the Republic. Michael Ancram will 'appear' on 'Primetime' as he did on 25 January, but not for an in-depth interview. The Irish media is not seen in Britain or read by any opinion formers there whom the NIO or Government Information Service wants to target. Watching this 'hierarchy of access' change in the last two years as control of events passed from NIO at Stormont to the Cabinet Office has been fascinating. Journalists from the North and the Republic have been virtually excluded from important briefings. The clearest evidence that the elections announcement was an ambush was that the *Belfast Telegraph* did not have Major's script. (Normally that paper would have an embargoed version available before the paper hits the streets at 12.30 pm.)

In the past year, extensive Downing Street briefings have been given on a regular basis to London-based journalists of British papers rather than to their Belfast-based correspondents. Thus there have been regular articles and analyses of the peace process by Hugo Young and Patrick Wintour of *The Guardian*, Stephen Castle and Andrew Marr of *The Independent*, and Andrew Bevins of *The Observer*. Apart from Hugo Young, these men have seldom if ever written on Ireland before 1994. The lobby system has also been used regularly to place items, however inaccurate. Although Belfast- or Dublin-based correspondents may object to the content, nevertheless, because the information has come from an MP or minister on a lobby basis, it usually gets printed. Leaks now go to the *Daily Telegraph* rather than to the *Belfast Telegraph*. Most recently the *Financial Times*, not a paper which has maintained an intense interest in Irish affairs, has been a favoured recipient of leaks. Again, all this reinforces the point that the British government wants to have its actions on Ireland legitimised by its 'own' media. But of course its own media is viewed and read by the majority of people in Ireland whom the British Government makes no effort whatsoever to influence. This places the Irish Government at a substantial disadvantage. David Miller concluded that massive resources 'give a significant advantage in struggles for definition'.[6]

The Irish Government cannot compete with the resources outlined at the beginning of this paper. But it can and should realise first that there is a struggle for definition being waged about each issue and even whether a topic is an issue. Secondly they should be aware of the limits of primary definition. Miller points out that it is limited by (a) the cohesiveness of the government; (b) the co-ordination of other organisations in the government; and (c) by the fact that the media can't be relied on to present government initiatives. As I have tried to explain, the first two limitations hardly apply at the moment since there is a greater unity on the British side now that the decision-making process has passed to the Cabinet Office. But the Irish Government can rely on the third limitation. The fact is the British media will give a fair hearing to alternatives to its own government's position. This is probably more likely to happen about Ireland than with any other item because the British Government's record on Ireland has been so much at fault. The dogged manner in which British journalists kept on about the Gibraltar shootings even to the extent of damaging their own careers is the best evidence for this. But the Irish Government and its press officers need to be aware of their audience and should pay attention to it in the acute manner of their British counterparts. The Irish media's audience is the whole island and producers do try to balance what they fear may be a nationalist line from southern politicians. To this end they regularly interview 'favourite' Unionists like Ken Magennis MP and Chris McGimpsey. For many Northern nationalists the regular appearance of these reasonable sounding men demonstrates either

6 Miller (1994).

ignorance on the part of southern broadcasters about the true position of Unionism or a forlorn belief among southern liberals that the Unionist leadership is as liberal as these two men. In 1994, Chris McGimpsey lost his position as honorary secretary of the party and in 1995 Ken Magennis was comprehensively defeated in the leadership contest. At last RTE woke up and now John Taylor MP, the Unionist party's deputy leader, regularly appears. But giving air time to Unionist views is not enough. RTE really does have to take into account that Northern nationalists, and some southern commentators too, expect to hear news bulletins containing an alternative to the spin coming from London through the BBC and ITN.

If RTE is sensitive to charges of nationalist bias on the North, equally the BBC and ITN or UTV are anxious to avoid accusations of Unionist bias. BBCNI and UTV have improved enormously over the past decade in their acceptance that there is a separate identity in the North apart from the British one. Coverage of GAA matches and feisanna is good. Broadcasting in Irish both on radio and TV is now commonplace. They do miss tricks, however. Both UTV and BBCNI ended their coverage of Clinton's visit as Air Force One lifted off from Aldergrove. There was an opportunity for Unionists in the North to see the Republic at work, hear Clinton in the Oireachtas and the speeches of Irish politicians. UTV and BBCNI missed it. On the other hand they have provided live coverage of the Forum for Peace and Reconciliation when Vice-President de Klerk addressed it. So there is progress.

The problem remains at London. BBCNI and UTV have no control over the output from there though they may groan at it from time to time. In London, broadcasters see the issue in the North as between two communities. They try to exercise balance. What they have not taken on board is that the two governments can also be at loggerheads, with the British Government a protagonist in the argument. It is a huge challenge. It requires a national TV or radio channel not to accept its own government's attempts at primary definition of an issue in dispute with a foreign government. What would happen in RTE if the news gave equal validity to the British Government's position alongside the Irish Government's view?

The problem is analogous to the phenomenon of parallax. The position of a star changes depending on the position of the observer. Or to take a more mundane example, and just to show there's no nationalist bias, let's take a cricket pitch. If you walk along the boundary, the wicket nearest you appears to move from, say, the left of the further wicket to the right of it. You need to take observations from at least two different points to find the true position of a star, or a wicket. The problem in dealing with Ireland is that there is no true position. There are two valid viewpoints no matter what position you look from: there are the British and Irish governmental positions and there are Unionist and nationalist positions. It is a tall order to ask national media to reflect that in their broadcasts, especially when they may have been given only one viewpoint from which to make an observation. A starting point may be for them to go and look up the concept of parallax and set it beside the concept of primary definition.

Let me finish as I started, with Lewis Carroll.

'Then you should say what you mean,' the March Hare went on. 'I do,' Alice hastily replied; 'at least—at least I mean what I say—that's the same thing, you know.'

'Not the same thing a bit!' said the Hatter. 'Why, you might just as well say that "I see what I eat" is the same thing as "I eat what I see!" '

The danger posed to democracy by the new media monopolies

DAVID BEGG

In recent times 'The Brady Bunch' has been enjoying a comeback on television. There are enough grey heads in the audience who, I am sure, like myself, remember this programme from the early seventies. Nostalgia for the sixties and seventies can be very seductive. 'The Brady Bunch' is a happy programme reflecting the comfortable lifestyle of middle America. Dad comes home from work dressed in a business suit, obviously a successful career man. He is greeted by Mom and Kids and they share their generally happy day. The main problem for the parents is how liberal they should be with the kids. Money is never talked about and is clearly not a problem. Middle America is a contented place.

Contrast this with 'Roseanne'. Roseanne and her husband Dan are fun people but they are constantly under pressure. Pizza is on the table a lot of the time. Dan is struggling with unemployment and tries one business idea after another. He has gone from opening a motorcycle repair shop to buying and renovating old buildings for resale. Roseanne has worked in a diner and eventually tries to open her own establishment selling loose meat sandwiches—whatever they are. They have constant difficulties with their children's relationships and indeed the extended family seems to be into various bizarre sexual arrangements. Roseanne and Dan are hard-working, if somewhat confused, people but they somehow cannot seem to get a decent run in life. Few people would want to emulate their lifestyle.

These contrasting images of middle America, set 25 years apart, are probably an accurate enough reflection of how people in this socio-economic grouping have seen their standard of living decline. America consists now of three categories of people: those on welfare who are constantly at risk of hardline Republican policies; those in the super-class bracket who have more money than they need and who live in

walled and guarded enclaves; and the middleclass who have just gone
through the floor. This change in the fortunes of the middleclass was at
the core of Pat Buchanan's campaign to become the Republican presi-
dential nominee and garnered him a lot of support which his conservative views might otherwise not have attracted.

Through programmes like 'The Brady Bunch' and 'Roseanne', television allows us to see very graphically the changing nature of society.
By any standards, television has been a powerful medium for information and for influence on society. The revolution now taking place in
information technology will profoundly alter society. There are those
who believe that the era of television is over. In a book titled *Life after
Television*, George Gilder argues that television and telephone systems—optimised for a world in which radio frequency spectrum or
bandwith was scarce—are utterly unsuited for a world in which, due to
advances in digital technology, bandwith is abundant. He says that TV
defies the most obvious fact about its customers—their prodigal and
effervescent diversity. People perform thousands of different jobs, pursue many various hobbies, read hundreds of thousands of publications.
TV ignores the reality that people are not inherently couch potatoes
and, given the chance, want to talk back and interact. By aiming its fare
at the lowest common denominator, television gets worse and worse
year after year. It will not survive an age in which linked computer systems can give a person interactivity and almost unlimited choice of
access to their own particular interest topic. If this comes to pass it will
be a great loss. I think Gilder is wrong about television. We need to
know what is happening to Dan and Roseanne. If we can insulate ourselves, via interactive computers, to only that view of the world we are
personally comfortable with, then we will become even more indifferent and selfish than we are at present.

The problem for anyone trying to make a judgment about the future
impact of structural change in the communications industry is that the
production of books making all sorts of extraordinary forecasts is a
growth industry in itself. It is something that needs to be approached
with caution; forming views or policy on the basis of one author's foresight can be a dangerous thing. Newt Gingrich is allegedly driven by
the view of the future contained in Hoffler's *Third Wave*. He now
stands as a less than totally credible figure in American public life.

Twenty-twenty hindsight is a more common phenomenon than twenty-twenty foresight. Nevertheless, it is already clear that changes in digital technology are causing the convergence of hitherto separate industries. The differences between telecommunications, computers, entertainment, and publishing are being progressively eroded and a new global communications industry is emerging. A new global market is being built on the back of this information technology revolution in which distance is less important than it was.

International conferences to discuss the changing nature of the communications world are now very popular in business circles. At one of them a former vice-president of AT&T, the huge American telecommunications company, told the following story: A theologian asked the most powerful supercomputer, 'Is there a God?' The computer said it lacked the processing power to know. It asked to be connected to all the other supercomputers in the world. Still, it was not enough power. So the computer was hooked up to all the mainframes in the world, and then all the minicomputers, and to all the personal computers. And eventually it was connected to all the computers in cars, microwaves, VCRs, digital watches and so on. The theologian asked for the final time, 'Is there a God?' and the computer replied: 'There is now!' It is a rather revealing story of the corporate mindset. One might even be justified in thinking it a little arrogant. But the fact is that we are on the verge of a world in which a small number of transnational corporations will dominate communications and these will have awesome economic and, by extension, political power.

Consider some of the recent developments in television. There has been a fierce debate in the British Parliament on Virginia Bottomley's Broadcasting Bill. The essence of it is whether satellite broadcasters like B Sky B should be allowed buy up exclusive rights to major sporting events, thereby excluding terrestrial channels like ITV and the BBC. The basis of the opposition to the proposal is that the enormous wealth of Rupert Murdoch would allow him outbid the others. This in turn would mean only selective access to the particular sport by those members of the public subscribing to the satellite station. Interestingly, the *Financial Times* Lex Column argued in support of the bill on the basis that it would allow sport to maximise the financial returns and this would be in the public good. But is it not a bit like arguing that

Croke Park or Lansdowne Road should be entirely set out in corporate boxes? A market is being created in which a virtual monopoly can control access to its product in such a way as to maximise the financial returns to itself.

Another interesting dimension to this argument is the relationship between B Sky B and the various cable companies in Britain. Most of these are owned by the so-called US 'Baby Bell' telephones companies like Nynex and US West. Fifty per cent of their product is entertainment and 50 per cent is telephony. It is an example of where interaction between formerly separate industries is taking place. On an international level some very heavy investments are being made. AT&T, the largest long-distance and international telephone company in the US, paid $137.5 million for a 2.5 per cent stake in Direc TV, a direct broadcast satellite television company. MCI, the second largest American telephone company, made a successful $682 million bid for a nationwide satellite television slot in the federal communications frequency auction. AT&T plans to develop integrated customer packages that will bring together Direc TV's entertainment programming, offered over the Direc TV satellite system, with long-distance, cellular, radio-paging and, in some areas, local telecommunications services delivered over its terrestrial infrastructure. The plans also involve the delivery of telecommunications and data services via satellite. Meanwhile, MCI, in which British Telecom holds a 20 per cent stake, will be able to offer a similar range of services to residential users, thanks to the relationship set up last spring with Rupert Murdoch's News Corporation. As part of this deal, under which MCI paid $2 billion for a 13.5 per cent stake in News Corporation, the two companies have set up a 50-50 joint programming venture.

In Britain, the link between telecommunications and entertainment giants is not as advanced. Nevertheless there have been contacts. BT is thought to have rejected an approach by News Corporation to take a stake in B Sky B in 1994, probably because of a fear of the political reaction. The current co-operation between BT and B Sky B followed the signing of a marketing deal between the two companies in November 1994. It involves the sale of satellite dishes through BT shops and the offer to B Sky B subscribers of two BT discount schemes for residential telephony. B Sky B also offers its customers favourable terms for subscribing to the cellular telephone service of Cellnet, 60 per cent owned by BT. This involves the use of B Sky B subsidies to provide free handsets and free connections. Cellnet commonly offers this type of discount in partnership with other companies.

In Germany, Deutsche Telekom is now being privatised and it has substantial investments (almost 20 per cent) in the Eutelsat series of satellites. It has acquired 25 per cent of its only worthwhile competitor, Aastra. Having a foot in both camps allows it to influence the policies of both competing organisations. Deutsche Telekom has also teamed up with Bertelsmann, possibly the largest media corporation in the world, and Kirch to form a company called Media Services. The object of Media Services was to dominate the market in the three areas of programme production, distribution, and supply. Because the European Commission ruled that Media Services would be an abuse of a dominant position, the company has gone away to reform itself so that it can meet the Commission's criteria. The key to Media Service's agenda was to develop and own a new encryption system for subscription television. In effect, it would be locksmith to the new system, so that anyone who wanted to gain entry would have to come to it for the keys. It would decide who could or could not have access to the network and decide what information got out to the public.

So, you will perhaps agree that even at this early stage of the convergence process very large and powerful multimedia corporate alliances are emerging. I refer to these as 'new monopolies' because their number and size are such that operating on a global basis they are, in practice, monopolies. They can be referred to as 'new monopolies' because they are replacing to some extent telecommunications companies which were established monopolies in the nation states they were established to serve. The difference is that the new monopolies are, firstly, global and, secondly, privately owned.

What can we say are the implications of these developments for civil society? The concept of the 'information society' suffers from being over-hyped as to what it can do for us. US Vice-President Al Gore, an enthusiast, said at one stage: 'If we had the information superhighways we need, a school child could plug into the Library of Congress every afternoon and explore a universe of knowledge, jumping from one subject to another according to the curiosity of the moment.' This assumes the library's books are all digitalised and available on the computer. They aren't; they never will be. Such claims for technology from highly placed political figures do not help us in arriving at a balanced judgment on the benefits and threats posed.

Opinion on the implications for democracy seem to be divided between those whose vision it is to live in a world where information is so comprehensive and the power for interactivity so sophisticated that every citizen can have an instant say in decisions and a sort of push button democracy. This would be a highly individualistic society in which people could exercise great control over their own lives. The alternative concern is related to the surveillance potential of information technology—a fear of an Orwellian Society based on the availability to the state of vast, interfacing computer data banks. This is a complex area beyond the scope of this paper. The question for now is whether these developments in the media threaten democracy.

Many people would, I think, be concerned by the lack of diversity in the newspaper industry in Ireland, particularly following the collapse of the Irish Press Group. If the communications industry becomes globalised as we anticipate and if news is controlled by a small number of transnational corporations, are we not likely to be at a very serious disadvantage? Will not public opinion, and hence political opinion, be shaped on a global basis in line with the views of those who control these communications corporations? What political party or government could stand up to the business aspirations of such corporations without being destroyed politically? Perhaps you feel this is overstating the position but, if so, how do you explain why Tony Blair found it necessary to pay homage at the News International conference in Australia last year. It must have been difficult for even the most fervent of 'New Labour' people to endure their leader bending the knee to the media mogul who played no small part in keeping them in the political wilderness for the past sixteen years. Similarly, did not the media empire of Silvio Berlusconi play a large part in the election last time of Forza Italia?

There is also the difficulty of regulating programme content and indeed there is difficulty in regulating what is on the Internet. How do you exercise any control on programme content that originates outside the state ? In an article in the *Irish Times* on 21 January 1996 Kathryn

Holmquist had this to say: 'Living in a video world with an international menu of pornography and violence at their disposal, certain vulnerable children are having greater and greater difficulty distinguishing reality from fiction. This isn't mere opinion: it is fact, based on research by Dr Nuala Healy and Marie Murray at St Joseph's Adolescent Services in St Vincent's Hospital, Dublin. Their study of Irish first-year pupils found that 41.8 per cent are watching TV to escape from the real world, and that 37.9 per cent are watching to block out pain. Their study of 1,000 12 to 17-year-olds found that more than two-thirds (70.9 per cent) had seen 17-cert sexually explicit videos and that half (49.8 per cent) believed that what they were seeing on video was "true life".' With 500 channels on TV and video on demand via interactive terminals, how will parents, even in the most stable families, exercise any control over what their children watch?

On the technical side, it is the twin forces of lower transmission costs and digitalisation that have propelled the liberalisation of the telecommunications and media markets and caused them to converge. As a result, a number of traditional media services, including broadcasting, can now be delivered efficiently by telecom networks. In a number of countries, cable companies are able to offer broadcasting and telephone along the same wires. This convergence raises more issues. Are the messages transmitted private or public and should they be controlled? Governments have always restricted broadcasters' freedom of expression in order to protect the public from harmful or offensive views. Telephone conversations, however, were left unrestricted because they were private. Into which category does the Internet fall ?

The increasing activity in the field of mergers and acquisitions in both telecommunications and broadcasting is a different form of convergence. How does one guarantee access to different service providers to ensure competition and a genuine plurality of views ? This issue of access to networks is critical where 'bottleneck' facilities are concerned, such as satellite transmission facilities. In many cases the owners of the networks also provide services, such as B Sky B, and they control whether their competitors get access or not. Is this a good situation to allow to prevail ? Indeed, with the development of new encryption systems for access to digital television services, this question becomes even more urgent.

It is one of the supreme ironies that the moves towards deregulation, rather than creating competition, have led to the creation of cartels of large multinationals which effectively control the communications industry. The protagonists for the totally free market have, to date, tended to dominate the debate about the communications industry generally and telecommunications in particular, and in that context regulation has become a dirty word. The free marketeers have argued that the availability of new and cheaper technologies obviates the need for regulation. It is critical now, at the time when the Irish Government is considering the regulatory framework it is going to introduce for telecommunications, that we actually have a proper debate on the question and do not slide into a policy simply through inertia.

The point was made very effectively by the Combat Poverty Agency in its submission on the Green Paper on Broadcasting—that access is the basic democratic issue. Access requires public control of the networks or the infrastructure of communications. But there is not necessarily a dichotomy between this objective and promoting competition. If infrastructure is of a high quality and accessible, then it provides a means by which the service providers can bring their products to the largest possible range of potential customers. Even in the past few weeks a very practical example of why some public control of infrastructure is desirable has emerged. New radio masts for the GSM mobile phone service are springing up all over the country. In the interests of the environment there should be just one set of masts with both ESAT Digiphone and Eircell co-operating in the use of them.

In summary, then, I believe that there are two issues upon which our government needs to act. Firstly, it should seek to influence the establishment of an international consensus on regulatory principles to apply to the emerging global communications industry with a view to ensuring that access and diversity are given equal weight to competition. The time is now opportune for this as the World Trade Organisation (WTO) is dealing with this topic at present. Secondly, it must ensure that the agreement reached on a strategic alliance for Telecom Eireann guarantees that the company will in the long term remain in majority public ownership. I say this because I do not believe that it is possible to ensure universal access to an expanding range of high quality communicating services unless Telecom Eireann continues to be an instrument of public policy. If the company becomes privately owned then all investment decisions will be driven by considerations of profit and will be directed east of a line between Dundalk and Cork. In such circumstances, the information superhighway for the rest of the country will be like our country roads, full of potholes!

Market forces have, it is quite widely believed, leaped free from government control and now control governments instead. Economic liberals hail such globalisation as the chariot of progress; democratic socialists fear that its scythed wheels are cutting down the hopes of socially beneficent intervention. The logic of the former view is that the world economy is dominated by uncontrollable global forces and has as its principal actors and major agents of change truly transnational corporations, which owe allegiance to no nation state and locate wherever in the globe that market advantages dictate. Those who applaud this development argue that the information society will empower individuals, diminish the importance of the nation state, and forever alter politics as we know it. In other words we will have a highly individualistic society. The problem is that if I am so secure in my information-rich world, then I don't have to care about anyone else, so why should anybody care about me ?

I have no doubt that there are huge benefits to be gained economically by the capability of information technology to reduce the effect of distance and peripherality. In the right circumstances, Ireland could be a real beneficiary of these advances. I am equally certain, however, that if governments don't find a way to effectively re-regulate it, society will suffer the consequences. I predict that, with the passage of time, governments will realise that their powers have been subverted and will seek to re-establish some measure of control. By then it may be too late.

The fault, Dear Brutus, lies not in the economic stars, but in ourselves that we make a mess of things.

Ownership, standards, diversity:
a way forward

COLM RAPPLE

Like motherhood and apple pie, a free and diverse media is on everybody's list of things desirable, although there is less agreement on what it means or how to achieve it. There is little doubt, however, that the trend is going in the wrong direction. The media is getting less free and less diverse. That adverse trend has been less pronounced in Ireland than in Britain, but it is there nonetheless. Competitive pressures have already put some newspapers out of business and others are at risk. All newspapers and the media in general are forced to adopt a more market-led approach to content. A wide range of news and opinion gets little coverage. An obvious example is the fact that the fairly even split in society over the divorce issue was not reflected in the media. There has been a tendency to ignore that very obvious and serious shortcoming. Many of those in the media prefer to forget it, while many of those who voted against divorce also prefer to keep quiet, afraid of being tarred with the fundamentalist, red-neck, dogmatic Catholic brush. The middle ground got lost somewhere along the way. But I digress. There are other and longer standing examples of exclusion from the media. For instance, one third of society—the social welfare class—has never had much access to the media. Unemployment, poverty, and the need to develop a real national consensus for tackling those problems get scant enough attention in our newspapers. Market forces are ensuring that that won't change.

In December 1995, a Ministerial Conference of the Council of Europe drew up a list of principles on journalistic freedoms and human rights. They are woolly enough but Principle One outlines the role of journalism in a democracy: 'The maintenance and development of genuine democracy require the existence and strengthening of free, independent, pluralistic, and responsible journalism. This requirement is reflected in the need for journalism to:

- inform individuals on the activities of public powers as well as on the activities of the private sector, thus providing them with the possibility of forming opinions;
- allow both individuals and groups to express opinions, thus contributing to keeping public and private powers, as well as society in general, informed of their opinions;
- submit the exercise of the various powers to continuous and critical examination.

The twin functions of newspapers in both informing the public at large of the activities of those in power and informing those in power of public opinion are well recognised in that principle. Irish journalists do comparatively good work in keeping tabs on those in power and reporting on their activities. But they are hamstrung by restrictions imposed by the laws on libel and official secrets, and they lack legal protection to allow them safeguard their journalistic sources. They lack other protections, too, and are faced with a narrowing field of potential employers. One must have reservations about the breath of the coverage—that is, the actual agenda of items considered worthy of reporting. A similar reservation applies in the case of the second function—that of informing those in power of public opinion or rather opinions because that is really where the diversity comes in. If it is to perform this role, the media must reflect the wide diversity of opinion existing in society and, of course, it should promote and encourage the formation of opinion by providing a channel for debate, analysis, and discussion.

The current debate on the newspaper industry in the Republic was sparked off by concerns over the expansion of Independent Newspapers, first through its acquisition of a 29 per cent stake in the *Sunday Tribune* and then its purchase of a 24.9 per cent stake in Irish Press Newspapers. The Minister for Enterprise and Employment, Richard Bruton, declared that the Independent wouldn't be allowed to increase its stake in the *Irish Press*, just as his predecessor, Des O'Malley, had ruled out any increase in the 29 per cent stake in the *Sunday Tribune*. It is the response one would expect within the context of competition policy and it is great as far as it goes. Movement towards monopolistic control is seldom in the public interest and should be curbed. But simply promoting competition will not ensure a free and diverse newspaper industry. Competition has reduced three evening newspapers in London to one. Not all that long ago there were 11 daily newspapers in New York. That's now down to three.

The situation is a little less clear in Ireland because there have been some new entrants. But the *Sunday Tribune* relies on cross-subsidisation from the *Independent* for its survival. That leaves the *Sunday Business Post*, which has carved out a sizeable niche for itself but, of course, three papers have disappeared from the market, victims to some extent of competition. The overall impact of competition has been to restrict rather than enhance diversity. The plain fact is that simple competition theory does not operate for newspapers. They are not simple products. They sell to two entirely different markets—advertisers and readers. In order to attract ads they must attract the right kind of reader. Advertisers are less worried about the quantity of readers than their quality. The ironic fact is that serious papers with sufficient editorial budgets to satisfy their journalistic role in a democratic society rely mostly on advertising revenue. Some 57 per cent of newspaper revenue in Ireland comes from sales and 43 per cent from advertising. But the split differs greatly from one newspaper to another. The *Irish Independent* is exactly on the average. The *Irish Times*, however, relies more heavily on advertising, which provides 58 per cent of its revenue. At the *Sunday Business Post*, it is even higher at 67 per cent. At the other end of the scale, the *Irish Press* relied on paper sales for a massive 80 per cent of revenue. Commercial pressures force all serious newspapers towards the centre. To maximise their advertising take they must attract the ABC1 category of readers—preferably in the big urban centres. There is no money in attracting poorer readers, who have tended to get short shrift as a result.

Noam Chomsky, professor at the Massachusetts Institute of Technology, has developed what he calls a 'propaganda model' based on a long study of the media. In his book *Manufacturing Consent* (New York, 1988), written in conjunction with Professor Edward Herman, he concludes that the media 'serve to mobilise support for the special interests that dominate the state and private activity, and that their choices, emphases, and omissions can often be understood best, and sometimes with striking clarity and insight, by analysing them in such terms.' He has a deep insight into the workings of the media. He does not suggest that there is any great conspiracy. It is more subtle than that: 'We do not use any kind of "conspiracy" theory to explain mass-media performance. In fact, our treatment is much closer to a "free market" analysis, with the results largely an outcome of the workings of market forces. Most biased choices in the media arise from the pre-selection of right-thinking people, internalised preconceptions, and the adaptation of personnel to the constraints of ownership, organisation, market, and political power. Censorship is largely self-censorship by reporters and commentators who adjust to the realities of source and media organisation and by people at higher levels within media organisations who are chosen to implement, and have usually internalised, the constraints imposed by proprietary and other market and governmental centres of power.'

What he is saying is that the media is so structured that dissent from conventional wisdom is limited. To become an issue, to be reported, to be built up as a major story, discussed, and taken seriously, a topic has to pass through a range of filters. Many topics, many important events, many developments just don't make it. He lists five filters affecting the American media but they would apply with some variation to the media in other countries:

- ownership;
- advertising;
- sources of information;
- flak — the reaction from powerful lobbies to those who transgress the norms;
- the ideology of anti-communism—this is the explanation for the support in the American media for military dictatorships in Latin America, for instance, on the grounds that a greater evil would be communism; so liberal ideas are tarred as communist and denigrated as such.

The reds-under-the-beds scare tactics are not as prevalent in Ireland anymore, although they were. I remember my own father being accused of being a communist and attacked in the *Catholic Standard* back in the 1950s when the first Yugoslav soccer team played in Dalymount Park. His sin was being secretary of Bohemians' Football

Club at the time. Philip Green refused to do a commentary on the
match and no band could be got to play the national anthems (not 'live'
in any case although one band did record the anthems). Claud
Cockburn reported that the then Lord Mayor of Dublin, Alfie Byrne,
spent the afternoon walking up and down O'Connell Street so that it
could be seen that he wasn't at the match. That's all a by-the-way. But
the old tarring tactic is still used. Commentators have been dismissed
as being Provo or even Democratic Left. That latter one is no longer
very effective now that the party is in government. But others are dismissed as being right-wing Catholics. Des Fennell, in an essay in his
book *Heresy*, describes how he believes certain new ideas are smothered
in Ireland with *silence* (a lack of response); *dismissal* as impractical or
irrelevant; and *excommunication*, with the author portrayed as a heretic.
He would seem to go beyond Chomsky's ideas, hinting at conspiracy
and I think that can be overstated. But there is no doubt that those with
original ideas or even with old ideas which don't fit into the establishment mould find it very hard to get them taken seriously, aired, and
discussed. If society is to progress, that needs to be changed. And one
way is to develop a more diverse media with greater access for all
shades of opinion.

Let us have a look at the other 'filters' outlined by Chomsky in an
Irish context.

Ownership is the issue that has been most addressed in the current
debate on Irish newspapers, but it would be very wrong to see it as the
only problem. Concentration of ownership will, of course, restrict
diversity and a wide spread of ownership will go a long way towards
providing a solution. But how do you prevent concentration?
Promoting competition, preventing takeovers, dismantling Independent Newspapers' dominant position in Irish-produced newspapers
may not in the long term leave us better off. It certainly wouldn't automatically create diversity. It is true that without the support of
Independent Newspapers the *Sunday Tribune* would collapse. It has
been claimed that the Irish Press titles might have survived had the
Independent been allowed to support them in the same way. Irish
newspapers face severe competition from Britain. Independent
Newspapers claims that the way to fight off that competition is to con-
solidate the Irish interests. If you take the total market for Irish news-

papers, it points out, the Independent group does not have a dominant position. But the Competition Authority has taken the view that the market is a segmented one. The market for Irish-produced papers must be seen as separate from the market for British-produced papers. The Independent does have a dominant position.

I must support that view and cast doubt on the *bona fides* of *The Independent* in its support for failing Irish newspapers. Its interest in the *Sunday Tribune* and the Irish Press titles can be explained as very strictly one of self-interest. Maintaining the *Sunday Tribune*, even at the cost of weekly subventions, makes financial sense in helping to keep out British competitors such as an even more Irish edition of the *Sunday Times*. It also helps to curtail the growth of the *Sunday Business Post* and the entry of a Sunday *Irish Times*. The 24 per cent stake in the Irish Press can now be seen as a defensive measure to keep out possible other investors who might have made a success of the three titles to the detriment of the *Irish* and *Sunday Independents* and the *Evening Herald*.

The demise of the Press titles has left Independent Newspapers in an overriding dominant position with about 70 per cent of the market for home-produced national newspapers. It controls two of the four daily papers produced in the state—the *Irish Independent* and the *Star*. They have an effective monopoly of the evening newspaper market; the *Evening Herald* is not really in competition with the Cork *Evening Echo*. Four Sunday newspapers are produced in the state, and the only one in which Independent Newspapers does not have a stake is the *Sunday Business Post*. It owns both the *Sunday Independent* and the *Sunday World* and effectively controls the *Sunday Tribune* through its 29.9 per cent shareholding together with substantial loans.

The Competition Authority has clearly set out the dangers of such a situation. In its first report on the *Sunday Tribune* stake it concluded: ' . . . the *Independent* could exercise an adverse and distorting effect on competition in the market. It could act in both a predatory and an exclusionary manner . . . It could reduce prices on a particular title, by means of cross-subsidisation, in order to weaken or eliminate a competitor. Controlling and having knowledge about its own three papers, the Independent might target a particular competitor and use both price and content as competitive weapons, in a contest which others which were already weak might find it difficult to survive. Editorial policy and advertising and the prices charges for advertising might be used to reinforce these strategies.'

In its more recent report on the *Irish Press* stake, it said: 'The concentration of ownership and control of newspapers and other forms of news media is particularly undesirable in a democratic society. Guarantees that editorial independence will be maintained are of limited usefulness where an individual or a single entity exercises some degree of commercial control over a number of competing newspapers. Indeed, such guarantees are virtually worthless and the only way in which independence can effectively be maintained is through diversity of newspaper ownership.' That has to be true, but having a diverse ownership is no guarantee of having a diverse media, and encouraging competition and outlawing anti-competitive activities will not necessarily promote diverse ownership. That is particularly so in an open market adjoining a larger country with the same language. There is one other danger in a concentration of ownership. It reduces the ability of journalists to resist commercial and other pressures by restricting their job options. In the new jargon, it disempowers journalists. I will return later to ways in which journalists might be empowered to better protect their professional standards.

Chomsky's second filter has to do with commercial pressures, in particular those imposed by advertisers. This is not just a matter of giving editorial plugs to advertisers or censoring out adverse comment about them or their products. That type of pressure is effectively blocked by most journalists on most national newspapers. But the need to attract advertisers in order to remain viable imposes a whole range of more subtle pressures. In particular there is the need to target those readers whom the advertisers want to reach and to create media packages that won't jar with the advertising.

The third filter through which news and comment has to pass before it gets into the newspapers comes under the general heading of sourcing. It has to do with how newspapers organise their news gathering, their relative lack of resources, and their need to rely on official and professional public relations sources. Those in the establishment who want to manipulate the media generally have more resources at their command than the media. And they are willing to use those resources. Public relations and spin-doctoring are lucrative businesses.

The best public relations practitioners and spin doctors don't tell lies; their job is more to set the agenda. Journalists and newspapers want news and they supply it but on their own terms. The newspapers need the PR men and women as much as they need the newspapers. Journalists face the same dilemma. Remember that most of what appears in our daily newspapers has been released by someone or other. Investigative journalism is a very small part of the total. Journalists have to produce copy. They have to have access to news sources. It is useful to have people who will package the news and present it to them. It can be disastrous to be frozen out. That can lead to a blinkered approach to what is news. It can sometimes be upset when a journalist from outside the speciality becomes involved.

Take the case of Gerard Ratner, who built a jewellery combine in Britain and indeed expanded into Ireland. His family business, the Ratners chain, was at the bottom end of the market but it was successful and went on the acquisition trail. It acquired H. Samuel and Weirs, among others. Gerard Ratner himself was a darling of the media. But what the media builds up it can also pull down. Indeed it seems to delight in doing just that. Mr Ratner was asked to speak at a management conference in the Albert Hall. He wrote his script, had a few friends look it over, made a few changes and presented it verbatim. I can only assume that he never showed it to a media professional. It contained a joke which was actually written in and distributed to the media in advance of the conference. It went something along the lines 'People ask me how we can sell our jewellery so cheaply. I tell them it's easy. It's because it's crap.' You know the result: lead stories in the tabloids. Gerard Ratner lost about £100 million and his job. The interesting thing is that he told the same story to a *Financial Times* reporter about a year earlier and it was printed in the middle of the interview without any repercussion. In that case the blinkers worked, and they generally do.

Newspapers with restricted budgets and limited resources need a ready supply of news, and the definition of news becomes distorted by what is readily available and by a certain degree of habit. That is why many topics of interest to the unemployed or other social welfare recipients get scant attention. But that's only one example. Another part of the same problem is limited access to the journalistic profession.

Few journalists come from poor backgrounds. This possibly reflects the fact that very few people from poor backgrounds manage to get a third level education, and that is changing only slowly. Indeed, more people from working/social welfare class backgrounds got into journalism 30 years ago than are getting in now. It was possible then to start as a copy boy and become an editor. It is very unlikely that it could happen anymore. The result is that the concerns of the poor get less than adequate attention in our newspapers. It is not the type of news that would attract the kind of readers that the advertisers want and few journalists can identify with the social welfare classes. Diversity would certainly require newspapers to provide more information for the poor and provide a greater platform for their views and concerns. For the most part, the poor are excluded from the Irish media and yet they comprise up to a third of the population.

Those are some of the factors working against the development of a free, independent, and diverse media. So how can they be counteracted? What is the way forward? There is no doubt that commercial pressures help to destroy diversity and encourage concentration. Simply promoting competition won't solve the question. The need for state intervention has long been accepted for the electronic media, so why not similar arrangements for the print media? It is certainly not a new idea. Various methods have been tried or suggested involving some form of subsidisation. It may be cross-subsidisation from one newspaper to another or some form of direct or indirect state subvention. It is possible to devise some automatic means of distribution of the subvention, which allows no room for discretion and therefore eliminates the risk of any element of state control.

These are not new problems and the suggested solutions are not new either. Back in the 1960s the British Government set up the Shawcross Commission, which heard a lot of suggestions. Unfortunately its recommendations were of the 'do nothing' variety. Nicholas Kaldor, the Cambridge economist, outlined how the market promoted concentration. He suggested a system of cross-subsidisation. The idea was to charge a levy on advertising revenue—the bigger the circulation the greater the levy. The resultant funds would be used to help papers with small circulations. The Young Fabians suggested a 40 per cent limit on the amount of space that could be used for advertising—not unlike the imposition on RTE a few years ago. But while RTE faced an absolute limit on the advertising it could take, the Young Fabians' idea would not prevent the more successful newspapers simply increasing their size and taking all the advertising offered to it. *The Guardian* suggested a progressive levy on newsprint, the rate rising with the tonnage used. The money would be redistributed to papers on the basis of editorial matter published—column inches by circulation. The idea was to penalise those papers that carried heavy advertising while subsidising editorial coverage. Since the pay-outs would be dependent on circulation, the market did have some input.

In the 1970s the British Labour Party put forward a very far-reaching proposal aimed at levelling the playing pitch for all newspapers, whether they were attractive to advertisers or not. Newspaper advertising would be channelled through a central board which would collect the revenue and distribute it to newspapers not on the basis of where the ads actually appeared but rather on the size of their readerships. Some of the money would also have been used to subsidise newsprint costs for low circulation papers.

Those were only suggestions and there were plenty more. We don't seem to have recognised the problem here in Ireland while many other countries have already moved to address them. Britain is not a good example to follow. In the end, it did nothing.

Many countries subsidise their newspapers. In France, there are three separate funds. In 1994, some £7 million was channelled through them. One fund helps French newspapers to expand abroad; another subsidises general and political interest daily national newspapers whose advertising revenue contributes less than 25 per cent of total revenue. A third fund helps local papers. TV advertising is taxed and the money used to subsidise newspapers and there are generous grants to help cover the cost of equipment. We are not talking about small amounts of money either. The TV tax yielded £9.4 million in 1994 while the equipment grants amounted to £34.2 million. French journalists also have a novel protection from the whims of their employers. Where a newspaper changes owners or editorial policy, the journalists have the right to opt for voluntary severance and receive a month's pay for every year of service. That is not bad in a country where there are diverse job opportunities.

Canadian newspapers, like Irish ones, face competition from a neighbouring country. But Canada has done something about it. Since 1976, Canadian companies are not allowed to claim tax relief on the expense of putting ads in foreign-produced newspapers or magazines available in Canada.

Those are some of the measures that can help to offset the commercial pressures that encourage concentration of ownership. Some such subsidisation and protections are needed in addition to competition laws aimed at controlling mergers and takeovers. Providing a more diverse media and a wider range of job opportunities must also strengthen journalists' commitment to their professional standards. A concentration of ownership and restricted job opportunities simply add to the pressures faced by journalists. Those pressures are very real. The Competition Authority had an understanding of the problem. On the matter of editorial charters and guarantees of independence in the context of the *Sunday Tribune*, it had this to say: 'At the end of the day the editor is constrained by commercial and financial considerations which can be conclusive. The editor may exercise self-censorship, deliberately or unconsciously. There may be direct interference by the proprietor, or influence may be imposed in more subtle ways and an editor may take heed of the proprietor for fear of losing his job. A charter can be changed, eliminated or disregarded. It could be effectively circumvented by dismissing a reluctant editor as is alleged to have happened elsewhere.'

Media diversity is a prerequisite for true democracy. A free market will not provide it, partly because of high entry costs, partly because of the dual markets, advertising and readership, which papers operate in, and partly because of economies of scale. There must be state intervention if there is to be diversity. Direct aid must be given to weaker publications but only in accordance with strict criteria that allow for no element of discretion. The criteria might include:

- an adequate editorial charter to ensure editorial freedom;
- a maximum circulation perhaps measured in terms of all the publishing group's titles in the relevant category—that is daily, evening, or weekly newspapers;
- a minimum circulation, to give the market some say;

- an acceptable ownership structure—perhaps even only to papers set up under a trust.

The funding could come either directly from the exchequer or from a levy on advertising revenue. If foreign-produced papers were net contributors to the subvention funds, so much the better. Another part of the package could be state intervention to ensure access for all to the most economical printing and distribution facilities—cross-subsidising low circulation publications particularly in distribution costs. But before we start devising a detailed package of intervention, we do need a clear statement of policy. It's over to the government on that one.

Church-media relations in Ireland: an onlooker's view

JOANNA BOGLE

'To see ourselves as others see us.' The poet reminds us of an uncomfortable truth—that from where we stand, we cannot see ourselves properly. We may look in a mirror, but things viewed there are notoriously back to front. We may look around us but that still puts us at the centre of the picture, unable to see it in perspective. In order to see ourselves as others see us, we have to invite someone else to do the seeing. I am that someone else. I am that 'other'.

In accepting the invitation to speak at the seminar, the stranger in your midst inevitably does so with some trepidation. In all our long history, too many Englishmen have arrived among the Irish as the strangers, viewing this island and its inhabitants, drawing conclusions, taking action. This visitor begins, I hope, with a sense of humility, and of history. For much of what we are going to discuss—Church/media relations in Ireland—is deeply embedded in a history in which the English are only too obviously involved. The present position of the Catholic Church in Ireland—its current tensions and difficulties, its specific problems with regard to the mass media—has its roots in a past in which persecution played such a significant role that it is impossible to ignore it. In order to tackle the reality of the present, it is essential to discuss the past.

I don't know if my own perspective, as an English Catholic journalist with my own tensions, contradictions, and history, is necessarily limited. I presume it is. But at least it is the 'other' view. A while ago, I was playing with my small niece Lucy and her dolls. 'What shall we dress Topsy-Mandy in now?' I asked, choosing among the little outfits strewn across the floor. 'This pretty white party dress?' 'That isn't a dress,' said Lucy, 'it's a nightie.' 'Are you sure?' I asked, holding up the puffed-sleeved garment with its pink frills and ribbons. 'To me it looks like a Sunday or party dress.' 'To Topsy-Mandy,' said Lucy with dignity, 'it looks like a nightie.' The way you see things depends on your viewpoint!

An invitation to an English journalist to speak to a media conference in Ireland might seem an invitation to a dance on eggshells. It is only because we can all have confidence in the traditional courtesies in this city of welcomes that it is possible at all. Thus when I refer to the appalling persecution to which the Catholic Church in Ireland was subjected for a long period of its history, and I add that this persecution was carried out largely at the behest of people from my country, with accents like mine, centred on a parliament meeting where mine now meets and in a tradition which is my own, you will know that this automatically imposes on me as the English visitor a personal sense of need to express sorrow and indignation. That the Catholic Church was also savagely persecuted in England, Scotland and Wales is not at this stage specifically relevant—what matters in Ireland is that it happened here, in huge measure and for a prolonged time, and has left the Church on this island with a specific burden of history.

It is a burden that it has borne in part with great honour. As an English Roman Catholic, I owe much to Irish priests and Irish nuns—working in our schools and parishes for the greater good of our common faith. And just as the priests and sisters went to England, so also they went all over the world to serve the emigrant Irish communities but also to serve the world in need, as missionaries, teachers, nurses, workers among the poorest people, in places far away from all that they had ever known and loved. This great missionary effort—driven in part by persecution at home and the consequent emigrations—is one of the great contributions to Irish, and world, history. But the persecution of the Church here had other effects besides driving people overseas. Much more prosaically, it created a Church driven in on itself. A Church which created its own defence structures, its own oddities, its own tensions and weaknesses. A Church which, perhaps inevitably, became over-clericalised, with power and authority vested in the priest. A Church which suffered from the lack of a well-funded, prosperous, and educated laity. A Church which, deeply rooted among its people and utterly interwoven with their lives and hopes and all that gives life meaning and purpose, did not and could not question and challenge itself. To outwit enemies, to strengthen and protect faith, to cherish a valued heritage, this all became second nature—and so it should, for survival is all-important if the Gospel is to be passed on from one generation to the next through the fragile mechanisms of a human community.

But today, Ireland's Church is in a completely different position. It is free, and has been for some generations. For much of this century, it has rested securely on its strong foundations, offering a confident, rock-solid picture to the world: Irish Catholicism. Laughed at or mocked, admired, noticed, accepted, the Irish Catholic priest with his faithful parish, his church packed to the doors umpteen times a Sunday, seemed a fixture on the scene. And then along came the 1990s and the whole thing seems to have been rocked to the core.

What happened? Conspiracy theory or hopeless confusion? The inevitable head-on collision between modern life and a decaying Church? Or a deep-rooted plan organised in some foreign capital city? Or a series of unconnected random events, faithfully reported by an unbiased media ? None of these things? Or a little of each? What caused the waves that are pounding today around the storm-tossed Irish Church in the media sea? Certainly the Irish Church was wholly unprepared for what was to hit it in the 1990s. The officers were on watch, the hatches battened down, but there had been inadequate attention to what was in the hold and even to the training of the crew. The heroism of the past—and the knowledge that the enemy lay beyond and not within—had caused a certain sentimentality to replace a more authentic spiritual discipline. And this in itself was a reaction to persecution too. One tragedy of Ireland's persecution was that academic study was restricted—Jansenism, or a certain puritanism, took root here because the wider learning that might have dispelled it was not available. The Jansenism was not, of course, restricted to Ireland, nor did it have its origins here, but anyone reading certain of the texts used for moral formation in the 19th and early 20th century cannot but be struck by a narrowness of tone and approach—incidentally wholly at variance with authentic Irish Catholic life and culture. There was a certain attitude which, ludicrous and absurd, utterly contrary to the traditional Catholic understanding of marriage and family, somehow came to be adopted—summed up in the story told to me by one Irish bride, now middle-aged, that 'of course you should turn the holy pictures round on your wedding night, to face the wall. It wouldn't be proper for them to see what goes on. . .' Wouldn't be proper? And yet the Church teaches us that the act of marriage is part of God's plan in which we share in His holiest of purposes, bringing new life into the world to share this life and eternity. She teaches that marriage is a sacrament, that children are a gift from the Lord. How can the Church, which cherishes the memory of Christ at Cana's wedding-feast, not see dignity and beauty in every Christian marriage? Perhaps in this wrong and nonsensical prudery something of the tragedy of today's unjust media treatment of the Church was born. For the alternatives to this prudery were either sentimentality—already mentioned and dangerous both because of its inherent mere reaction to Jansenism and because of its complete lack of intellectual depth—or an enthusiastic leaping into the 'liberal' sexual attitudes which swept European and American culture in the 1960s and 70s and are now well entrenched.

And it has been the whole question of sexual behaviour on which the Church/media tension has centred: the Irish nation debating about divorce, abortion, contraception; the Church, upholding what is true and unchanging, yet apparently crudely and hopelessly undermined by the devaluing of these sacred truths by sexual misbehaviour on the part of some of the clergy. The scene was set for an inevitable battle.

In fact, that scenario is not an entirely accurate one. Only a tiny minority of Ireland's clergy—and of England's, and America's, and Austria's, and so on—have strayed from their path of commitment to the Christian teaching on sexual purity and restraint. The vow of celibacy has been widely honoured, and lives poured out in service to God and community in total faithfulness and dedication to the fullness of Catholic teaching. So the picture we have been given of a Church at variance with itself between preaching and practice is not really a true one. And yet the world cannot but take its images from the media, which is the artist which paints them for us.

To the English observer, the treatment the Catholic Church gets in today's Irish media seems crudely and cruelly biased. There is something ludicrous about it; there is a manic flavour. 'Aha!' it seems to be saying viciously, 'so you thought this was boring old Ireland, did you, persecuted and virtuous, poor but cheerful, downtrodden but full of whiskey and blarney? Loyal to Mother Church and only too ready to honour her traditions, reverence her clergy, and accept her principles? Well, you're wrong. We're . . .er. . .well. . .modern. And secular. Oh, my gosh, yes, secular. None of that Catholic stuff. Oh, gosh no. That was all a lot of hooey got up by Bing Crosby in the movies, and used for oppressing women and usurping the freedoms of the population generally. So there.'

Now this may be very understandable. It may be a reaction against Jansenism. It may be a frustrated reaction to a wider world's sneering. It certainly has something in common with the current British obsession in which we question our monarchical traditions, ceremonies, constitutional arrangements, and so on. It is a reaction to being laughed at, a way of tackling at once the envy and the sneers of the world. But is it truthful and honest? And does it communicate an authentic sense of identity, an accurate interpretation of where most men and women of this nation are, and what they are thinking and saying? An intelligent media, in both Britain and Ireland, could be taking a cool and useful look at the Church at this stage of Ireland's history. But sadly instead the media seems to be relishing every current scandal, and gleefully anticipating more to come. There seems to be a lip-smacking pleasure in the idea of a once-proud Church now toppling to its knees. The Bishop Casey scandal and then the horrific abuse of children by some other clergy as proven in court should have opened up an overdue and necessary discussion, but seems instead to have degenerated into something cynical and somehow artificial. My impression is that people dislike and resent it. They know that there are profound issues to be tackled, which aren't being tackled at the level they deserve.

In many ways, the mass media—in Ireland, in Britain, across Europe, in America and Australia—is in very much the position of power and authority it often claims the Church is in: having a hold over people's imaginations, setting the agenda for debate, holding itself morally aloof as it announces a point of view or denounces a sinner! We need a much more critical analysis of the media, its power, and influence. Pornographic magazines, TV and videos have undoubtedly played a part in the fostering of a rather sex-obsessed society of which sinful priests are also a part and in no small sense are victims. Why should the mass media smugly point and sneer when a sexual sin is revealed—when the media's own pornographic images, sexual innuendo, blatant support for immoral lifestyles, failure to treat things with modesty and decency, have all been part of the problem? Few and brave are the voices in today's mass media which speak for marriage as the lifelong commitment at the heart of society, which tell the truth about the link between homosexual behaviour and the killer disease AIDS, which publish the truth about the misery caused to teenagers by the provision of contraceptives for them and the subsequent rise in out-of-wedlock births and shattered lives.

Where is the TV programme that has pointed to the crude and often inaccurate material pushed at children and young people in the name of 'sex education', often publicly funded by taxation (for instance, in Britain, through the Health Education Council)? Where is the honest debate on the effects of no-fault divorce on British society? Where is the flow of information, ideas, criticisms, and challenging, thought-provoking discussion on the plight of the thousands of children being brought up in divided families who never see their fathers? These are huge areas for public debate—ignored and lost, while headlines sneer at the Church and hint at 'more dark scandals to come' in Ireland and elsewhere.

When we look at the Church and the media, we are entitled to ask about these things. We are entitled to speak for the marginalised, for the ordinary people whose values and lifestyles are the ones that keep society going, that pass on cherished wisdom to the young, that nurture family life, that are the only real line of defence against crime and viciousness. And this is happening at a critical time in Irish and European history. The Christian faith, around which European civilisation has been based and without which that civilisation will most certainly perish, is fading from our common life and culture. The acquisition of material goods, the dominance of a worldwide pop culture through which millions of the world's youth tune in to a universal sound, the sense of instantaneous wishes (food, sex, fun, entertainment) instantly gratified—all this challenges the older framework of a life in which messages and values were transmitted across the generations and through a myriad of means, including folklore, family, traditions, and culture. So Ireland, where the Christian faith has played such an extraordinarily central role, is caught up in this wider struggle. This should be an exciting time to be a media commentator, a newspaper columnist, a TV interviewer. Instead, there is little to be seen of this sensitive and dynamic reporting of news or commenting thereon. But instead, we see merely a superficial approach, analogous to the comments of a delighted teenager who, chafing under parental restraint, thrills with pleasure when Mum and Dad in turn get into trouble with authority for some misdemeanour. Deep down, he knows that their parenthood still holds authority and meaning but meanwhile it is fun both to sermonise at them and to sneer at their discomfiture. Unknown to him, or at least unnoticed or deliberately ignored, the very fabric of his home and the bonds that draw its members together are under threat. While it is fun to point to parental misdeeds, the children go astray, the elderly relatives are neglected, neighbourly and civic duties get abandoned, the rot sets in.

In case you think I am simply here to sneer at and attack Irish newspapers, radio and TV, let me emphasise that of course I do not pretend to know them as I know those of my own country. And I have to say that some of the ways in which the Irish Catholic Church and its beliefs have been presented in the British media has been atrocious. I think of a BBC Radio 4 'Today' morning radio programme some while back, tackling the divorce issue, which gave an atrociously one-sided interview in which just one viewpoint was presented—that supporting divorce—and a wholly distorted presentation was made of Irish life and attitudes. In fact, it was so bad that our Minister for Agriculture, who happened to be interviewed next about something to do with beef or pig-farming, actually began his own interview by saying 'I simply must comment on the appalling distortions and injustice in that last item about Ireland!' And I personally would venture to add that things are often said and alleged about Ireland or Irish ways, especially Catholic ways, that would be deemed racist or unacceptable if said about another nation or religion.

Incidentally, on the divorce issue, I cannot but add briefly my own plea in this capital city: that Ireland does not follow Britain's cruel and unjust divorce laws. In Britain now, you can be divorced against your will, and robbed of your home and children, with no effective legal redress. The media, Parliament and the wider public are just beginning to wake up to some of the grave injustices that have been perpetrated in British courts over the past few years. Here is an issue for the Irish media to tackle: come and talk to us, to the lawyers like my husband who practice in the family courts and see what goes on there, to the groups such as Families Need Fathers and other networks which try to help broken men to pick up the pieces after their lives have been shattered. Above all, tell the truth, and on this side of the Irish Sea, let justice prevail. To any injustices she has given Ireland over the years, don't let Britain add her hideous and cruel anti-family ideology of recent decades.

So there is my overview as an English visitor. 'To see ourselves as others see us.' This is how we see you: staunchly Catholic but over-sensitive about not looking modern and sexually liberated, anxious to 'catch up' with a Europe and an America which have been dancing to a jaded party tune for some while now and are actually rather bored and exhausted. Slightly apt to think that 'modern' means somewhere in the 1970s. A little scared on tackling the challenges of the next century, and yet in reality holding the key: for this island's ancient faith is surprisingly supple and strong, has endured through far greater changes than those we have seen in this century, is far older than 19th century statues and sentimental hymns, and holds unchanging truths about the very core issues of life itself. I think I would echo Pope John Paul's words in Poland: 'Be not afraid!'

Cleraun Media Conferences

The papers in this volume were delivered at the Sixth Cleraun Media Conference held in Dublin on 24-25 February 1996. The title of the conference was 'Good Morning, Ireland: do the media wish to inform us, entertain us, or change us?' The contribution of those who chaired the sessions of the conference is gratefully acknowledged. They were:

HUGH DUFFY
Chief Executive, Irish Music Rights Organisation

PETER FEENEY
Editor of Current Affairs, RTE

MICHAEL FOLEY
Media Correspondent, *Irish Times*

CHRIS LENNON
Political Correspondent, *Irish Independent*

DR COLUM KENNY
Lecturer in broadcasting at Dublin City University and columnist with Independent Newspapers

SENATOR ANN ORMONDE
Fianna Fáil spokesperson in the Seanad on education and enterprise and employment

DR IVO O'SULLIVAN
Chairman, Family and Media Association

DAVID QUINN
Editor of the Irish Catholic and columnist with the *Sunday Business Post*

RICHARD ROCHE
Head of the Department of Journalism and Media Studies, Griffith College, Dublin

The contribution of M. Hubert Astice of the Ministry of Culture in Paris, and of the French Embassy in Dublin, is also gratefully acknowledged.

The conference was held in Cleraun, 90 Foster Avenue, Mount Merrion, Co Dublin—a study centre and hall of residence for third-level students which is an apostolic undertaking of Opus Dei, a prelature of the Catholic Church.

Previous Cleraun Media Conferences have looked at a broad range of topics including ethical issues in news reporting, coverage of conflict, and advertising; the media on terrorism, violence and crime; the use of broadcasting bans by government, including the views of a US journalist who was a hostage in Lebanon; opening access to the airwaves and community radio; investigative journalism; the Church and the media; regional versus national press, media education.

Index